200 Years of

Political

Campaign

Collectibles

Mark Warda

GALT PRESS
Clearwater, Florida
www.galtpress.com

First Edition, 2005

ISBN 1-888699-02-7
Library of Congress Catalog Number: 2002117629

Manufactured in the United States of America.

Published by Galt Press, a division of Galt International, Inc., Post Office Box 8, Clearwater, Florida 33757-0008. This publication is available by mail for $29.95 plus $4.30 shipping plus Florida sales tax if applicable. For credit card orders call 727.581.8685, or email galt@galtpress.com.

Dedication

To my wife, Alexandra, who, to my pleasant surprise, enjoys political campaign items almost as much as I do.

To my parents, James and Jennie Warda, who kept politics interesting by nearly always taking opposite sides of an issue.

To the late Professor Milton Rakove of the University of Illinois, from whom I took many of my Political Science classes and who advised me that a law degree would be more useful than an advanced degree in Political Science.

To Mayor Richard J. Daley's Chicago political machine, which taught me the reality that the best candidate doesn't always win, the best organized one does.

To Richard M. Nixon, who taught me that you don't always know a candidate until long after an election is over.

To the next popular and charismatic president our country finds, whoever he or she may be.

Acknowledgments

Thanks to Mark D. Evans, APIC member #995, who provided valuable help with editing and pricing. Any errors must have been added after he reviewed the manuscript.

Thanks to Tom Slater of Slater's Americana who allowed me to use many photographs from his comprehensive political auctions.

Thanks to Kirk Mitchell and the family of J. Harold Cobb for permission to us photos from his collection of George Washington buttons.

Thanks to Al Anderson, of Anderson Auction who helped complete the list of hopeful presidential candidates.

Thanks to Harvey Goldberg, Kurt Hurner, and Alex Miller who shared pictures of items in their collections.

Thanks to the American Political Items Collectors organization which has provided much useful reference material over the decades and continues to help collectors build their collections. For more information see Appendix 1.

Contents

Part II - Collecting Political Campaign Items

Mouse Pads
Comb
Telephone Cord
Seat Cushion
Chimney Flue Cover
Bed Pan
Bank
Yo-yo
Fly Swatters
Sewing Needles
Tatoos
Frisbee
Paper Cube
Antenna Ball
Coin Pouch
Fishing Lure
Light Switch Cover
Candy Jar

Introduction

The artifacts of American political campaigns document the development of the greatest experiment in the history of mankind. While other human cultures have promoted allegiance to the state or to a religion, America is the first society dedicated to the freedom of the individual. This freedom has allowed us to become the most prosperous and successful society of all time.

But the goals of Americans have not always been the same and freedom of others hasn't always been everyone's goal. While some campaigned to free slaves others campaigned to prohibit alcohol. While some campaigned to give every citizen the vote, others campaigned to tax the income of those citizens who made more than other citizens. These issues that Americans fought for and against have been the subject of countless buttons, pamphlets, posters, banners and other ephemera. These items were usually discarded when a campaign was over, but those that survived show us the colorful history of American politics.

By studying the campaign items from the last 200 years we can also learn that the issues in the campaigns were not all that different from those of today, that the concerns of our grandparents were the same as some of our concerns. Supporters of President William McKinley wore buttons in 1896 demanding "Sound Money" and today many Americans want to "Balance the Budget." Supporters of President Franklin Roosevelt in the 1930s wanted a social security program. Today many people want to save that program from possible bankruptcy.

This book offers a history of memorabilia from over 200 years of American political campaigns. It is meant to be useful to the historian, the collector, and those who just want to learn more about how Americans over the years felt about politics.

While the historian may be offended by putting a price on history, the collector is eager to know what an item for his collection will cost him or what an item he discovers is worth. Since this book is about collectibles, there is a need to let the reader know the relative values of the items shown. To better understand the pricing of political items, see the next page and *How Much to Pay for Items*, page 92.

The hobby of collecting political campaign items is relatively young. While surely some people saved political buttons and trinkets since the first George Washington inauguration, the hobby of collecting political items was not formally organized until 1945 and the first catalogs were not published until the 1960s and '70s. Compare this to stamp and coin catalogs which have been available for over 150 years.

Collecting political campaign items is not like collecting coins or stamps. Those are issued by the government and production records are carefully kept. Every variety has been cataloged and values are easy to determine. Political campaign items have been produced by thousands of private companies, local committees and even individuals. For most items there is no record of how many were made or where or how they were distributed or sold. New items are being discovered every year and we will probably never know all of the designs and varieties.

Because of this factor, the hobby has become very addictive for many collectors. The excitement of finding an unknown item at a flea market or getting a $1000 button for $10 at an antique store has many collectors traveling the country, checking every flea market, trolling the Internet, and scouring every possible source for political items.

Hopefully, this book will be of help.

Prices

Political collectibles are not as easy to price as collectibles such as stamps or coins. Those hobbies have millions of collectors and there are good stocks of most items available. If you want the rarest Lincoln penny, a 1909-S VDB, you could call half a dozen coin dealers and most would have one in stock and the prices would be nearly identical. If you wanted a button from the same year, for example a 1909 Taft inaugural button, you might have to search for it for months if not years, and six different dealers would give you six different opinions of what it is worth, some of which might be double or triple what the other dealers said.

With fewer items available and fewer collectors chasing them, the prices of political items are very flexible. A rare button might sell at an auction for $1000, but six months later a similar one might sell for $600 or $1500, depending on how many of them have come to market recently and how many collectors are actively looking for it. If no collector is actively looking for a certain $1000 item for his collection, there is always a dealer or a collector looking for a bargain who will pay $500 to $800 for it. If two wealthy collectors need that item to complete a part of their collection, they might bid it up to $1500, just so they don't have to spend another year or two looking for it.

The prices in this book are given in ranges. As a buyer you will know that if you got it at the low end of the range you got a good deal, and if you got it at the high end you didn't overpay. As a seller, you will know that if you sell at the low end you got a fair price, and if you sell at the high end you got a good price. Of course, because of the flexibility of the market, you will sometimes be able to buy at lower than the low end and sell at higher than the high end.

Since this book covers 200 years of political items in less than 200 pages, it can only picture a fraction of what is available. If, say, a political token is priced at $50 to $100, that price covers most tokens of that type. But there may be exceptions, such as an especially rare design that can sell for $1000. As explained in the chapter on pricing, you need to follow the auctions if you want a more precise idea of what an item may be worth at the time.

The publisher may issue price updates for this book in the future. For information send an email to 200years@warda.net.

Disclaimer: The author's company manufactured some of the recent political items pictured in this book for sale during the campaigns (1992-2004),but all estimated values have been reviewed by an outside expert.

Numbering

Because some collectors like to refer to a specific item pictured in a book, we have included a numbering system. Each item on a page has a different letter next to the price, so to refer to a specific item you can say "200 Years, page 40-P," or just "40-P."

Part I - History of Political Campaign Items

This first section of the book shows campaign items for each president since George Washington, and for most runners-up. Also included are some of the political cause campaigns such as women's suffrage and prohibition.

Since there was not a popular election for our first president, most of the items are souvenirs from his inaugurations. Since he was a war hero, there were some items from that period of his life. There are also memorial items, but items issued after a president's death are of much less interest to collectors than those made during their lives, especially their campaigns.

For the next several elections, from 1796 through the 1820s, most states had their legislature choose their presidential electors. When the states started allowing their citizens to vote for the electors in the 1820s, more items began to be issued promoting presidential candidates.

The first mass market campaign was in 1840 when people all over the country got involved in the election. This was the first election in which most Americans knew what their candidate looked like! It was an exciting and vigorous campaign and many types of pro- and anti- campaign items can be found for both sides of the campaign.

From then onward many types of items were distributed to promote presidential candidates in every election. Medals worn on the jacket were among the first. Then came paper pictures under glass with pewter rims, ribbons, flags, booklets, paintings under glass, clocks, mugs, pitchers, dishes, posters, and ballots that could be brought to the polling place and dropped in the ballot (in case you couldn't read or write). Some uniquely 19th century items were snuff boxes with the candidate's picture, lantern slides to be shown at rallies, parade torches, and complete parade uniforms emblazoned with the candidates' names and pictures.

In 1894 the celluloid button was patented, allowing an attractive design to be made into a durable campaign button. This began the golden age of political buttons which lasted until the 1920s when the button designs were mostly black and white, or sepia.

After the dull designs of the 1920s, buttons began to get more and more colorful, and today they are as graphic as ever, sometimes even including electric lights or moving parts. Some of the designs of the 1890s have even been recycled into buttons for the current campaigns.

In each election, new consumer items were made into campaign pieces. There are pocket watches, chimney flue covers, matchstick holders, horse bridle fasteners, buggy whips, automobile license plate attachments, bumper stickers, pot holders, trivets and coffee scoops. More recently there are yo-yos, paper cubes, telephone cords, and even campaign mouse pads.

For the first hundred years covered in this book, items of all types are included on the pages for each candidate. Collectors usually collect whatever they can find from this era because there are so few items available. For some collectors, items that fit into a standard display case as more desirable than bulky items.

For the second hundred years there are many attractive buttons and stamps, so most collectors concentrate on those items. For other types of items for the more recent elections see Part 2 of the book where they are listed in their own categories.

1789 - 1792 George Washington

The first American political items were made to commemorate George Washington's inauguration. The most common of these were metal coat buttons, and Washington himself was said to have worn buttons picturing eagles on his coat. But there were also some cloth and ceramic items made for the occasion. These have always been popular collectibles, but they were not actual campaign items, used to determine an election. Rather they were mementos of the event. There were also many Washington items made during his life and shortly after his death.

A   15,000-20,000

Many of the available buttons are in rough condition, since they were dug up by people scouring the Northeast with metal detectors. Because they are so desirable, even rough specimens command hundreds of dollars.

Reproductions of these have been made since at least 1876 to celebrate the Centennial of American Independence, so you should be careful when buying. The best way to buy is from a reputable dealer who will guarantee authenticity.

B   300-600

C   1000-1500

D   1000-3000   E   1000-3000   F   800-1500

G   20,000-25,000   H   5,000-10,000   I   15,000-20,000   J   4000-7000

Beginning in the 1950s, J. Harold Cobb put together the most complete collection of George Washington buttons ever assembled. He also kept detailed records on how many were known of each item, who owned them, and where they were first found. In 1968 he published a booklet on his findings. His collection was left to his family and in early 2003 it was sold through Stack's, a New York coin company. The prices realized for the best pieces were astronomical and may not be accurate values for future sales.

His family has put photographs of his collection on the Internet including an updated version of Mr. Cobb's book which can be downloaded and printed. The web site is here:
http://moscow2.pld.com/kirk/CobbGW/index.html

1796-1820 John Adams through John Quincy Adams

Very few items are known for our second through sixth presidents, most likely because few were made. In those days the presidential electors were chosen by state legislatures, rather than by a vote of the people, so campaign items were not needed. Most items from those years celebrated a sitting president.

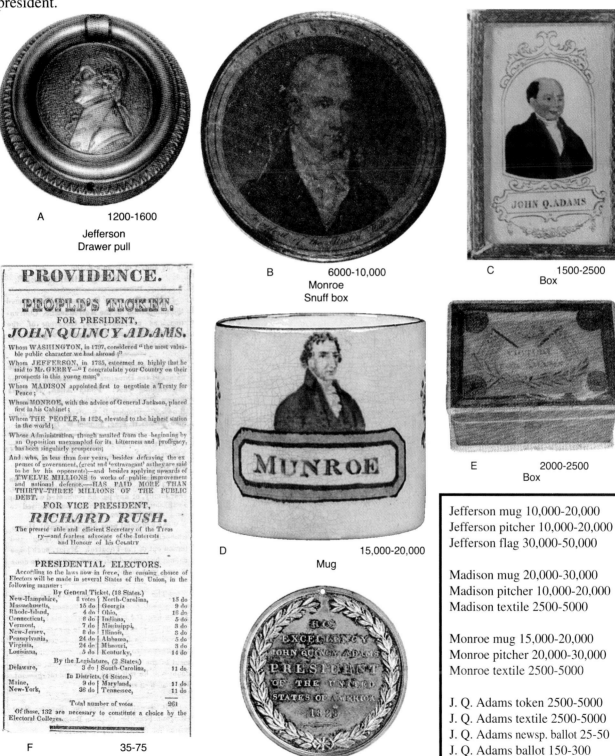

A   1200-1600
Jefferson
Drawer pull

B   6000-10,000
Monroe
Snuff box

C   1500-2500
Box

E   2000-2500
Box

D   15,000-20,000
Mug

F   35-75
Newspaper ballot

G   3000-4000

Jefferson mug 10,000-20,000
Jefferson pitcher 10,000-20,000
Jefferson flag 30,000-50,000

Madison mug 20,000-30,000
Madison pitcher 10,000-20,000
Madison textile 2500-5000

Monroe mug 15,000-20,000
Monroe pitcher 20,000-30,000
Monroe textile 2500-5000

J. Q. Adams token 2500-5000
J. Q. Adams textile 2500-5000
J. Q. Adams newsp. ballot 25-50
J. Q. Adams ballot 150-300

1824 - 1832 Andrew Jackson

The Andrew Jackson tokens from 1824 are considered the very first presidential campaign items. He wasn't nominated in that election but was elected president in 1828 and 1832.

A   3000-5000
Reverse painting on glass

B   700-1200

C   2000-2500

E   100-150

F   150-300
Button with Jackson
name on back

D   2000-4000
Snuff Box

G   2000-4000
Snuff Box

Jackson snuff box 2000-4000
Jackson mug 2000-4000
Jackson pitcher 3000-5000
Jackson plate 700-1200
Jackson flask 300-600
Jackson bandanna 1500-3000
Jackson textile 1000-2000
Jackson ribbon 1500-5000
Jackson token lg. 500-1000
Jackson token med. 400-800
Jackson token sml. 100-300

THE PATRIOT.

CONCORD, APRIL 28, 1828.

National Nomination,

Made by the States of New-York, New Jersey,
Pennsylvania, Maryland, Virginia, South
Carolina, Georgia, Tennessee, Alabama,
Mississippi, Louisiana, Missouri, Illinois,
Indiana, Kentucky, and Ohio.

FOR PRESIDENT,

ANDREW JACKSON.

FOR VICE PRESIDENT,

JOHN C. CALHOUN.

I   30-60
Newspaper ballot

H   60-100

J   15-30

1836 - 1840 Van Buren vs. Harrison

There are very few items known to be from the 1836 campaign, but in the 1840 rematch between Van Buren and Harrison, the number campaign items exploded. While there were only about 70 tokens and medals made for all candidates from 1824 through 1836, there were at least 150 made just for Harrison in 1840. This was the first mass market campaign. While Harrison actually had a prosperous upbringing, both his supporters and detractors pictured him as having come from poor roots, and the log cabin and cider barrel were the symbol of his campaign.

A   1500-2500

B   1500-2500

C   1000-1500
"Sulfide"

A, B, + C: Brooches

D   75-125
Button

E   40-80
Button

F   100-150

G   40-80

H   30-60

I   6000-8000
"Sulfide"

K   3000-5000
Pewter-rimmed
picture

J   4000-6000
"Sulfide"

L   75-150

M   5000-7000

N   2000-3000
Snuff Box

O   4000-6000
Brush

P   150-300
Hand-colored print

Harrison snuff box 2000-3500
Harrison plate 200-1000
Harrison sml. glass dish 75-125
Harrison pitcher 2000-4000
Harrison flag 5000-10,000
Harrison bandanna 2000-4000
Harrison ribbon 200-600
Harrison sulfide 1000-8000
Harrison jacket button 50-300
Harrison token lg. 200-500
Harrison token med. 75-200
Harrison token sml. 20-50

Van Buren ribbon 1000-3000
Van Buren snuff box 2000-4000
Van Buren flag 20,000-30,000
Van Buren brush 6000-9000
Van Buren sulfide 4000-8000
Van Buren jacket button 200-400
Van Buren token lg. 500-1000
Van Buren token med. 300-500
Van Buren token sml. 50-150

1844 Polk vs. Clay

Prior to the 1844 presidential campaign the expectant candidates, Van Buren and Clay got together and made an agreement not to discuss the possible annexation of Texas during the campaign. However, Van Buren was not nominated and Clay's ambiguity on the issue probably cost him the election to Polk who supported annexation.

Henry Clay was the man who said he would rather be right than be president. He may or may not have been right, but he was considered a contender for the presidency at least 6 times from 1828 to 1848.

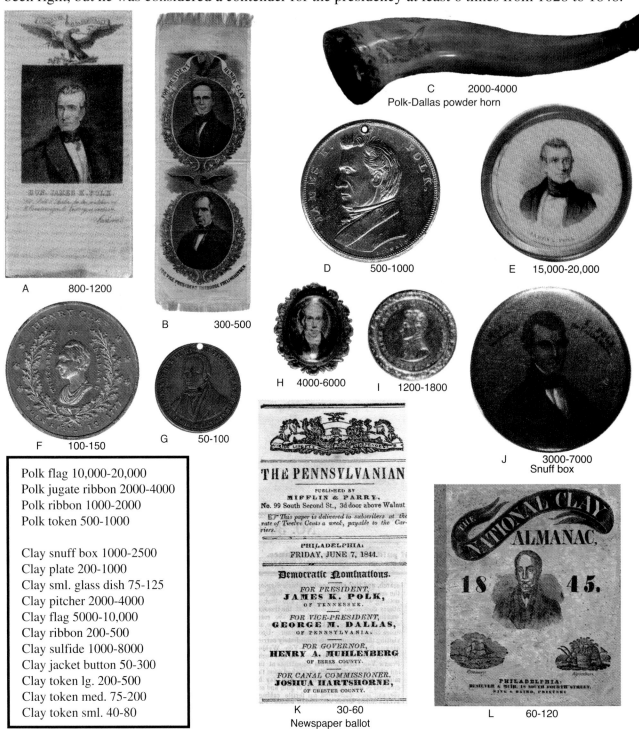

A   800-1200

B   300-500

C   2000-4000
Polk-Dallas powder horn

D   500-1000

E   15,000-20,000

F   100-150

G   50-100

H   4000-6000

I   1200-1800

J   3000-7000
Snuff box

K   30-60
Newspaper ballot

L   60-120

Polk flag 10,000-20,000
Polk jugate ribbon 2000-4000
Polk ribbon 1000-2000
Polk token 500-1000

Clay snuff box 1000-2500
Clay plate 200-1000
Clay sml. glass dish 75-125
Clay pitcher 2000-4000
Clay flag 5000-10,000
Clay ribbon 200-500
Clay sulfide 1000-8000
Clay jacket button 50-300
Clay token lg. 200-500
Clay token med. 75-200
Clay token sml. 40-80

1848 Taylor vs. Cass and Van Buren

A hero of the recent war with Mexico, General Zachary Taylor easily won the election against Democrat Lewis Cass and former President Van Buren running on the Free Soil ticket. Perhaps because of his military fame and having died in office, Taylor items are not as rare as others of the era.

A   4000-6000

B   10,000-12,000
Pewter-rimmed picture

C   1500-2500
Snuff box

D   50-100
Button

E   200-400

F   800-1200

G   15,000-20,000
Pewter-rimmed picture

H   1000-1500
Ribbon

I   50-100

J   300-600
Soldier's shaving mirror

K   2000-3000

L   20-40

Taylor snuff box 1500-2500
Taylor mug 500-1500
Taylor ribbon 1000-2000
Taylor mourning ribbon 200-400
Taylor bandanna 2000-5000
Taylor textile 200-400
Taylor flask 200-800
Taylor jacket button 50-300
Taylor token lg. 300-600
Taylor token med. 100-200
Taylor token sml. 75-200

Cass ribbon 1000-2000
Cass token 200-500

1852 Pierce vs. Scott

General Winfield Scott of Mexican war fame beat out President Millard Fillmore (who took office on President Taylor's death) for the Whig nomination, but lost to Democrat Franklin Pierce. Items for both candidates are relatively scarce.

A   100-150

B   200-400
Pipe

C   80-120

D   50-100
Campaign biography

E   50-100
Ticket

F   150-250

G   50-100   H   50-100

I   75-125

J   50-100

Pierce flag 10,000-20,000
Pierce ribbon 1000-2000
Pierce token lge. 250-500
Pierce token med. 150-250
Pierce token sml. 50-150

Scott flag 10,000-20,000
Scott ribbon (jugate) 3000-5000
Scott ribbon 500-1000
Scott token lge. 250-500
Scott token med. 150-250
Scott token sml. 50-150

K   15-30

L   15-30

1856 Buchanan vs. Fremont and Fillmore

James Buchanan, the last Democratic president for 28 years, beat both Fremont, the first Republican presidential candidate and former President Fillmore.

A   1200-1800

B   50-75

C   50-75

D   40-60

E   200-400

F   25-50

G   30-60

H   30-60
Stamp

I   2000-3000

J   1000-2000

K   200-350
Cloth broadside

L   20-40

Buchanan flag 10,000-20,000
Buchanan bandanna 2500-4000
Buchanan jugate ribbon 1000-3000
Buchanan ribbon 300-1000
Buchanan token lge. 500-1500
Buchanan token med. 100-300
Buchanan token sml. 50-150

Fremont flag 10,000-20,000
Fremont bandanna 2000-3000
Fremont jugate ribbon 1000-2000
Fremont ribbon 200-500
Fremont token lge. 250-500
Fremont token med. 100-200
Fremont token sml. 50-100

Fillmore flag 10,000-20,000
Fillmore jugate ribbon 1500-2500
Fillmore ribbon 500-1000
Fillmore token lge. 2000-3000
Fillmore token med. 100-200
Fillmore token sml. 50-100

1860 Lincoln vs. Douglas, Breckinridge and Bell

While items for all the candidates in the four-way race of 1860 are prized, Lincoln items are of course the most sought after. Lincoln's 1860 items can be distinguished from his 1864 items because he was beardless in 1860.

A   300-600

B   400-600

C   200-400

D 400-800

E   75-150

F   2000-2500

G   1200-1800

H   250-400

I   1000-1500

J   15,000-25,000

Envelope

K   60-120

Lincoln flag 6000-30,000
Lincoln jugate ribbon 5000-8000
Lincoln ribbon 1000-3000
Lincoln token jugate 500-800
Lincoln token lge. 300-800
Lincoln token med. 100-200
Lincoln token sml. 50-100

Douglas flag 5000-25,000
Douglas jugate ribbon 2000-3000
Douglas ribbon 1000-2000
Douglas token lge. 200-400
Douglas token med. 100-200
Douglas token sml. 50-100

Bell flag 10,000-20,000
Bell ribbon 2000-3000
Bell token lge. 200-400
Bell token med. 100-200
Bell token sml. 75-150

L   300-500

M   20-40

O   50-100

P   50-100
Stamp

N   30-60

Breckinridge flag 10,000-20,000
Breckinridge ribbon 2000-3000
Breckinridge token med. 200-400
Breckinridge token sml 50-150

Q   15,000-25,000

1861 Davis and Stephens

Jefferson Davis items are very rare and are missing from most political collections. But they could be included in a collection of American presidential material because Davis was elected president of seven of the United States. Davis items are highly prized by Civil War collectors. Since stamps and currency picturing Davis were issued during his term of office, they can be considered contemporary items, rather than memorial items like U. S. postage stamps picturing dead presidents.

A   1500-2500

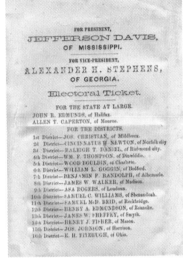

B   150-300

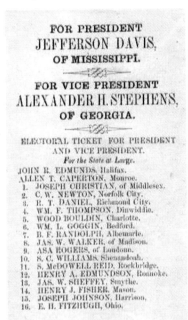

C   150-300

D   150-225
Envelope

E   40-60

F   20-40

G   40-60

1864 Lincoln vs. McClellan

With a civil war going on, political feelings were strong and a great number of items were made for this election. Lincoln's are more common because his assassination made him a martyr. Even though more people collect Lincoln items, McClellan's are often more expensive.

A   300-600

B   400-800
Ferrotype photo
pinback

C   300-600

D   100-200
Cardboard photo
pinback

LORAIN COUNTY.
OHIO
UNION PRESIDENTIAL TICKET
(Election November 8, 1864.)

For President,
ABRAHAM LINCOLN,
OF ILLINOIS.
For Vice President,
ANDREW   JOHNSON,
OF TENNESSEE.

Electors.
JOHN M. CONNELL, } At Large.
JOHN P. BIEHN,
JOHN K. GREEN,
STANLEY MATTHEWS,
LEWIS B. GUNCKEL,
STEPHEN JOHNSTON,
WILLIAM L. WALKER,
MILLS GARDNER,
HENRY W. SMITH,
OZIAS BOWEN,
JACOB SCROGGS,
WILLIAM SHEFFIELD,
GEORGE A. WALLER,
HENRY F. PAGE,
JAMES R. STANBERY,
JOHN H. McCOMBS,
FREDERICK W. WOOD,
LORENZO DANFORD,
JOHN McCOOK,
SETH MARSHALL,
ABNER KELLOGG.

E   40-80

Flag   G   6000-12,000

H   75-150

F   1000-2000

I   2000-2500

J   200-400

K   200-300

M   300-600

N   3000-5000
Paper lantern

L   200-400

Lincoln bandanna 5000-10,000
Lincoln paper lantern 500-2000
Lincoln envelope 50-100
Lincoln jugate letterhead 75-200
Lincoln ballot 75-150
Lincoln newspaper ballot 20-40

McClellan flag 8000-15,000
McClellan ribbon 500-2000
McClellan token lg. 100-200
McClellan token med. 75-125
McClellan token sml. 50-100
McClellan ballot 75-125
McClellan newspaper ballot 20-40

O   100-200
Letterhead

P   100-200

1865 - 1868 Andrew Johnson

Since Andrew Johnson was never a nominee for president there are relatively few items for him. The most popular items are tickets to his impeachment trial. Only a few years ago these were available in the $100-200 range, but now they are usually $500-1000 and more. A real challenge would be to assemble a complete set. Although the trial took place from March 23, 1868 through the day of the vote, May 16, 1868, it was supposed to start earlier and last longer so tickets are available for many more dates.

A   300-500

B   75-150

C   100-200

D   75-150

E   150-225

F   1000-2000

G   300-1000

H   100-500

I   25-50
CDV

J   25-50
CDV

K   150-300
Sheet music

L   150-300
Poster

1868 Grant vs. Seymour

Since Ulysses S. Grant was a war hero and a popular president, his items were saved by many people and are not exceptionally rare. Horatio Seymour items are much harder to come by.

A   400-700

B   300-600

C   75-125

D   100-200

E   150-225

F   250-400

G   300-500
Ribbon

H   20-40

I   300-500

J   300-400

K   150-250

L   75-150
Black rubber
token

M   300-500

N   200-300

O   250-400

Grant flag 5000-10,000
Grant paper lantern 300-600
Grant ribbon 200-500
Grant sheet music 75-150
Grant envelope 50-100
Grant token lg. 100-200
Grant token med. 75-125
Grant token sml. 30-75
Grant rubber token 75-125

Seymour flag 5000-10,000
Seymour ribbon 500-800
Seymour envelope 30-60
Seymour jugate letterhead 40-80
Seymour token lg. 100-200
Seymour token med. 75-125
Seymour token sml. 30-75

P   100-200

Q   20-40

1872 Grant vs. Greeley, et al

Items which are clearly from Grant's second campaign are hard to find. Items for Greeley, who died a few weeks after he lost to Grant are very rare and highly sought after.

A   2000-2500

B   400-600

C   300-400
Paper
lantern

D   15,000-20,000

E   3000-4000

F   700-1200

G   800-1200

H   75-150

I   400-600

K   20,000-25,000
Banner

THE PEOPLE'S TICKET.

FOR
President,

FOR
Vice President,

HORACE GREELEY.   B. GRATZ BROWN.

The unanimous choice of both
the Liberal Republican and
Democratic Parties.

J   200-400

L   75-125
Signature

M   500-1000

N   150-200
Pair of CDVs

(Grant prices on previous page.)
Greeley flag 5000-10,000
Greeley bandanna 1500-2500
Greeley ribbon 500-1000
Greeley fan 500-1000
Greeley token lg. 100-200
Greeley token med. 75-125
Greeley token sml. 30-75

1876 Hayes vs. Tilden

Items from 1876 are among the toughest of the era. The election was a virtual tie and decided in the House of Representatives by a political deal in which Hayes, who received fewer popular votes than Tilden, was selected the winner. Like in the 2000 election, some Democrats considered the election "stolen."

A   300-600

B   500-800

C   150-250

D   2000-3000
Poster

E   150-200

F   400-700

G   75-150

H   800-1500

I   100-200

J   40-80
Stereoview

K   40-80

L   500-800

M   500-800

N   100-200
Newspaper error: "Tilden won"

O   40-80

Hayes flag 5000-10,000
Hayes bandanna 1000-2000
Hayes ribbon 200-500
Hayes token lg. 100-200
Hayes token med. 75-125
Hayes token sml. 30-75

Tilden flag 5000-10,000
Tilden bandanna 1000-2000
Tilden ribbon 200-500
Tilden token lg. 100-200
Tilden token med. 75-125
Tilden token sml. 30-75

1880 Garfield vs. Hancock

Because Garfield was assassinated and Arthur became president, their items were saved by many more people than saved Hancock items. Thus the latter are much scarcer. But since presidents are in more demand, the values are similar. Garfield memorial items are much less desirable than campaign pieces.

A   250-500

B   15-25

C   50-100

D   50-100
Poster from Harpers Weekly

E   800-1200

F   40-80
Sticker

G   75-150
Sticker

H   20-30

I   600-1000

J   150-250
Oilcloth ribbon

K   30-60

L   30-60

Garfield flag 5000-10,000
Garfield bandanna 100-300
Garfield ribbon 200-500
Garfield token lg. 100-200
Garfield token med. 75-125
Garfield token sml. 30-75

Hancock flag 5000-10,000
Hancock bandanna 100-300
Hancock ribbon 200-500
Hancock token lg. 100-200
Hancock token med. 75-125
Hancock token sml. 30-75

1884 Cleveland vs. Blaine

Cleveland was the first Democratic president elected since 1856. Items for both Cleveland and Blaine are relatively common and inexpensive. Since Cleveland ran three times it is hard to identify some items with a particular election. Those with Hendricks as his running mate are from 1884.

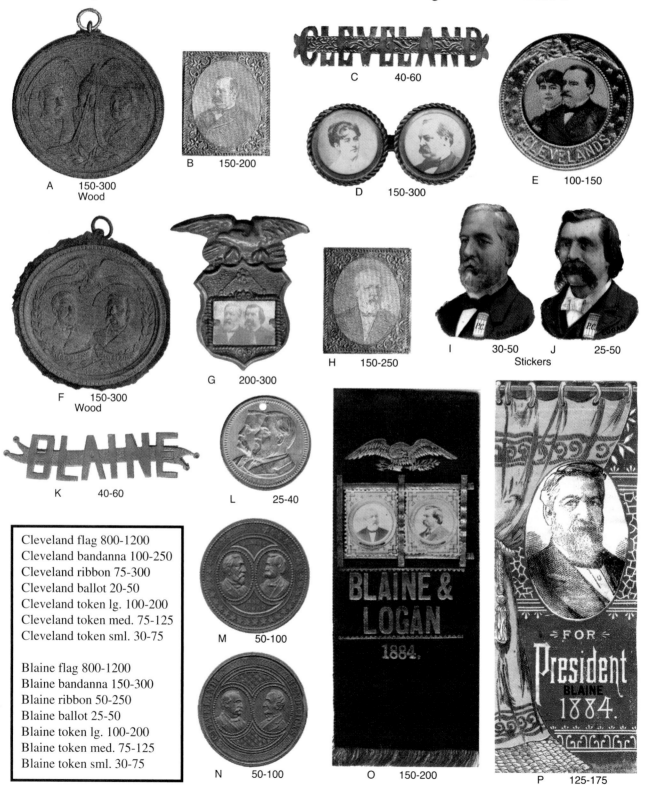

A   150-300
Wood

B   150-200

C   40-60

D   150-300

E   100-150

F   150-300
Wood

G   200-300

H   150-250

I   30-50   J   25-50
Stickers

K   40-60

L   25-40

M   50-100

N   50-100

O   150-200

P   125-175

Cleveland flag 800-1200
Cleveland bandanna 100-250
Cleveland ribbon 75-300
Cleveland ballot 20-50
Cleveland token lg. 100-200
Cleveland token med. 75-125
Cleveland token sml. 30-75

Blaine flag 800-1200
Blaine bandanna 150-300
Blaine ribbon 50-250
Blaine ballot 25-50
Blaine token lg. 100-200
Blaine token med. 75-125
Blaine token sml. 30-75

1888 Harrison vs. Cleveland

Although President Cleveland received more popular votes, he lost to Harrison who won more Electoral College votes, as happened in the 2000 election. There are many varieties of items from the 1888 election including matching items that were produced by vendors for both candidates.

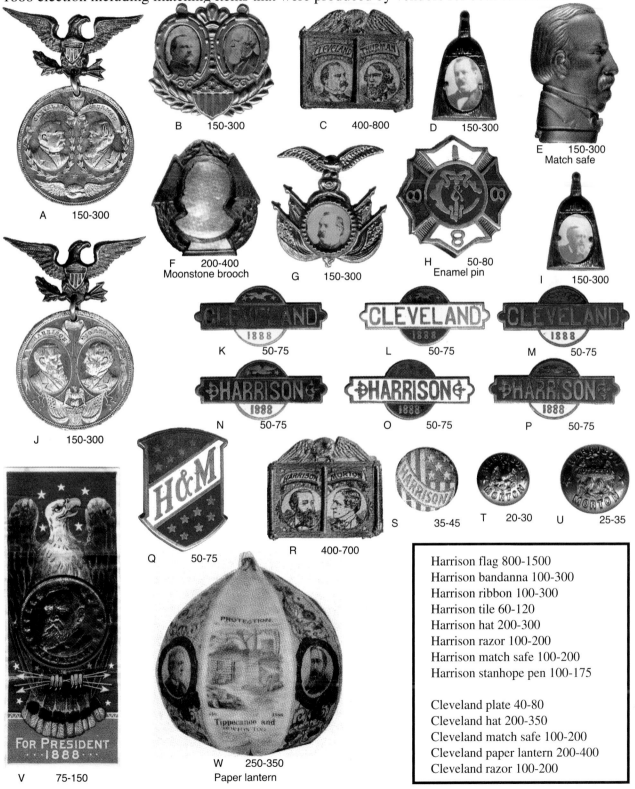

A   150-300

B   150-300

C   400-800

D   150-300

E   150-300
Match safe

F   200-400
Moonstone brooch

G   150-300

H   50-80
Enamel pin

I   150-300

J   150-300

K   50-75

L   50-75

M   50-75

N   50-75

O   50-75

P   50-75

Q   50-75

R   400-700

S   35-45

T   20-30

U   25-35

V   75-150

W   250-350
Paper lantern

Harrison flag 800-1500
Harrison bandanna 100-300
Harrison ribbon 100-300
Harrison tile 60-120
Harrison hat 200-300
Harrison razor 100-200
Harrison match safe 100-200
Harrison stanhope pen 100-175

Cleveland plate 40-80
Cleveland hat 200-350
Cleveland match safe 100-200
Cleveland paper lantern 200-400
Cleveland razor 100-200

1892 Cleveland vs. Harrison Rematch

The 1892 election was the only time in American history that a defeated president came back and won an election. Items that are clearly from the 1892 election are harder to find than those from the two previous elections.

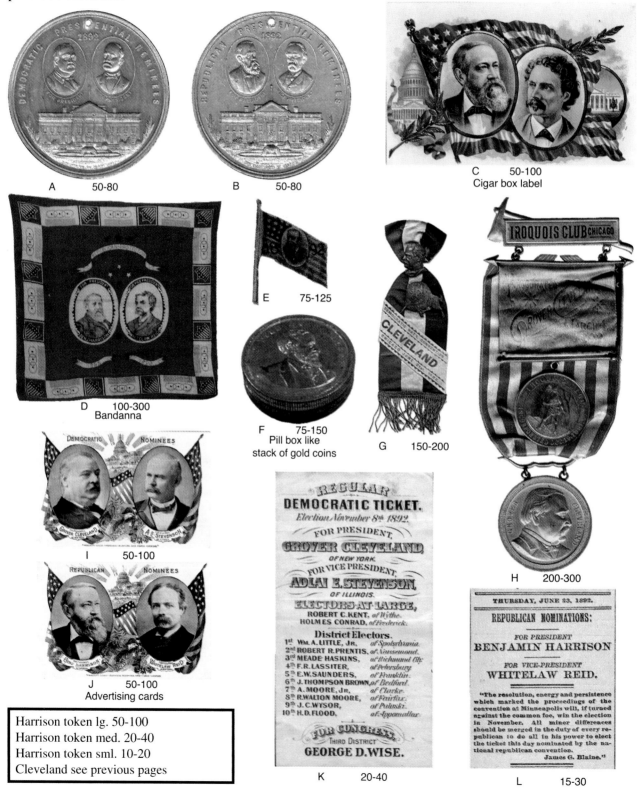

A   50-80

B   50-80

C   50-100
Cigar box label

D   100-300
Bandanna

E   75-125

F   75-150
Pill box like
stack of gold coins

G   150-200

H   200-300

I   50-100

J   50-100
Advertising cards

Harrison token lg. 50-100
Harrison token med. 20-40
Harrison token sml. 10-20
Cleveland see previous pages

REGULAR
DEMOCRATIC TICKET.
Election November 8th 1892.
FOR PRESIDENT
GROVER CLEVELAND
OF NEW YORK.
FOR VICE PRESIDENT
ADLAI E. STEVENSON
OF ILLINOIS.
ELECTORS AT LARGE,
ROBERT C. KENT, of Wythe.
HOLMES CONRAD, of Frederick.
District Electors
1st WM. A. LITTLE, JR., of Spotsylvania.
2nd ROBERT R. PRENTIS, of Nansemond.
3rd MEADE HASKINS, of Richmond City.
4th F. R. LASSITER, of Petersburg.
5th E. W. SAUNDERS, of Franklin.
6th J. THOMPSON BROWN, of Bedford.
7th A. MOORE, JR., of Clarke.
8th R. WALTON MOORE, of Fairfax.
9th J. C. WYSOR, of Pulaski.
10th H. D. FLOOD, of Appomattox.
FOR CONGRESS,
THIRD DISTRICT
GEORGE D. WISE.

K   20-40

THURSDAY, JUNE 23, 1892.

REPUBLICAN NOMINATIONS:

FOR PRESIDENT
BENJAMIN HARRISON

FOR VICE-PRESIDENT
WHITELAW REID.

"The resolution, energy and persistence which marked the proceedings of the convention at Minneapolis will, if turned against the common foe, win the election in November. All minor differences should be merged in the duty of every republican to do all in his power to elect the ticket this day nominated by the national republican convention.
James G. Blaine."

L   15-30

1896 - 1900 McKinley vs. Bryan

The elections of 1896 and 1900 were the beginning of the "Golden Age" of political campaign buttons. Those were hotly contested elections and the country was excited about politics. Well, most people were; see item "F" for people who had enough of all the political excitement.

One of the big issues of the day was whether to allow the free coinage of silver. Silver interests in the west wanted their silver to be valued at one-sixteenth of the value of gold. Thus their slogan was "16 to 1" and their candidate was the Democratic nominee, William Jennings Bryan. The Republicans preferred to stick with the gold standard. Thus most silver buttons of the time supported Bryan and gold buttons supported McKinley. Supporters were called "gold bugs" and "silver bugs" and wore insect pins in those colors.

A   200-300

B   60-80

C   100-125

D   50-75

Full Dinner Pail

The "full dinner pail" was a symbol of the Republican party and appeared on several buttons of the era. The Democratic answer was a dinner pail with the bottom fallen out of it, or the slogan "the empty dinner pail." (Some, if not all "empty dinner pail" items might be from 1904 or 1908.)

Crown of Thorns

Bryan's most famous speech, which is still known as one of the most moving speeches in American history, is his "Cross of Gold" speech in which he implored that a crown of thorns not be pressed "down upon the brow of labor" and that mankind not be crucified "upon a cross of gold." This inspired several buttons and even some real thorns painted gold and attached to ribbons to be worn as campaign items.

E   100-200

G   2500-5000

F   40-60

H   40-60

I   2500-5000

Buttons in the designs of "C," "D," "F," "I," and "J," were made in several sizes and for both parties (with gold backgrounds for Republicans and silver for Democrats). It is a challenge to get each design in each size but several collector have done it.

A   200-300

B   150-250

C   40-60

D   40-60

E   40-80

F   40-60

G   40-60

H   20-30

I   20-30

J   20-30

K   6-12
Sticker

L   10-20

M   75-150
Parade badge

N   50-100

O   60-100

Since William Jennings Bryan ran for president three times (1896, 1900 and 1908) it is hard to distinguish which buttons are from which election. Button "A" has such a young photo it must be from 1896. Button "B" matches McKinley buttons from 1900 so it is likely from then. Jugates are easy since his running mate was different each time. Button "C" pictures Stevenson, his running mate in 1900. For some 1908 Bryan buttons see page 36.

A 60-100

B 50-100

C 100-150

D 3000-5000

E 2000-3000

F 8-15

G 75-125
(Anti-Bryan)

H 50-75
Tobacco tag

I 25-50 J 25-50 K 25-50 L 25-50

M 10-20
Sticker

N 1000-1500
Serving tray

O 800-1200
Flask

P 1500-2500
Umbrella

Teddy Roosevelt

After the assassination of President McKinley in 1901, Teddy Roosevelt became both the new president and an American icon. A "Rough Rider" in the Spanish-American war, a big game hunter in Africa, and a rebel who started his own political party when he disagreed with the Republican party, Roosevelt captured the center stage of the era. During the 1912 campaign he was the target of an assassination attempt but went on to give his speech before having the bullet removed from his chest.

Teddy Bears

There is some dispute as to how the "Teddy Bear" originated. The most likely story is that it started when President Roosevelt went on a hunting trip in which not many animals were encountered. Finally a bear was sighted, but it was so young that Roosevelt refused to shoot it. When the story circulated, political cartoonist Clifford Berryman illustrated the incident for the papers. Morris Michtom, a Brooklyn candy store owner whose wife made bear dolls, saw it and asked Roosevelt for permission to call them "Teddy Bears." Permission was granted, the company took off to become Ideal Toy Company, and the Teddy Bears became ubiquitous.

A   200-300

B   200-300

C   100-200

D   10-20
Poker chip

E   800-1200
Pinback with moveable mouth

F   40-60
Post card

G   25-40

H   40-60

I   50-80
Carrying a "big stick"

J   100-200

1904 Roosevelt vs. Parker

As popular as Roosevelt was, there weren't many Democrats eager to take him on in the 1904 election. The task went to Judge Alton B. Parker of New York who lost in a landslide.

A   175-225

B   150-200

C   200-300

D   200-300

E   150-200

F   100-150

G   10-20 Stamp

H   200-300

I   300-600

J   300-600

K   100-150

L   40-80

M   50-75

N   60-90

O   60-90

P   75-125

Q   100-150

R   40-60

S   60-90

T   75-125

U   100-150

1908 Taft vs. Bryan

When Roosevelt left the presidency in 1909, Taft was his chosen successor. Bryan was nominated a third time by the Democrats. Items for both candidates are plentiful and relatively inexpensive.

A   10-20
Post card

B   200-300

C   600-1000

D   15-25
Paper tab

E   40-60

F   75-125

G   20-30

H   40-60

I   1000-1500

J   30-50

K   25-40

L   20-30

M   100-150
Tip dish

N   10-20
Post card

O   25-40
Fob

P   500-1000

1912 Wilson vs. Roosevelt and Taft

When Teddy Roosevelt returned to America from his world travels, he was not happy with the policies of his chosen successor, President Taft. He tried to retake the nomination but Taft had the party machinery locked up. So Roosevelt quit the Republican party, started his own party, the Bull Moose, or Progressive party, and split the Republican vote, allowing Wilson to win.

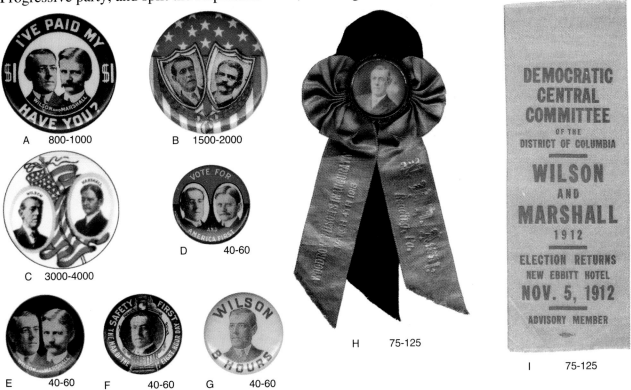

A   800-1000

B   1500-2000

C   3000-4000

D   40-60

E   40-60   F   40-60   G   40-60

H   75-125

I   75-125

Since Taft ran with Sherman in both 1908 and 1912 it is hard to tell which Taft items are from which year. Many can be found dated 1908 but few are dated 1912. Those which match Wilson and Roosevelt designs, such as "L" are known to be from 1912.

L   100-150

J   50-100

K   250-400

M   75-125

N   200-300

Teddy Roosevelt's Bull Moose Party

Teddy Roosevelt's new party was called the Progressive, or Bull Moose party. The bull moose was chosen as the party's mascot. Some believe it was related to Roosevelt's saying that he felt "fit as a bull moose" but it is also claimed to be named after Roosevelt's friend, Edwin A. Merritt, speaker of the New York Assembly who was known as Bull Moose.

A   200-300

B   60-90

C   4000-6000

D   2500-3500

E   1800-2300

F   30-60

G   40-60

H   40-60

I   25-40

J   25-40

K   15-30

L   100-150

M   10-20

N   20-40

O   25-40

P   100-200

Q   150-300

R   40-60

1916 Wilson vs. Hughes

Some thought the third party campaign by former Republican President Teddy Roosevelt was the only reason a Democrat, Woodrow Wilson, could capture the presidency. When the 1916 election came around, the candidacy of a former Supreme Court Justice, Charles Evans Hughes, was expected to return the presidency to the Republicans. One newspaper even headlined Hughes as the winner of the election (before all votes were in). But the Democrats took advantage of American patriotism during the first world war and asked citizens to "Stand By the President."

A   10-20
Stamp

B   150-250

C   800-1000

D   40-60

E   400-600

F   200-300

G   100-200

H   75-100
Post card

I   50-75
Post card

J   50-75
Fob

K   40-60

L   40-60

M   10-20

N   15-25
Stamp

O   5-10

1920 Harding vs. Cox (and Roosevelt)

The 1920 election is known by political collectors for two things, the most plain and unattractive buttons of any year and the "holy grail" of all political buttons, the Cox-Roosevelt jugate. Since most buttons were in black or sepia, colorful ones are the most sought after.

A   100-200

B   250-350

C   200-250

D   500-800

E   80-120
Harding
mechanical
nose thumber

F   1500-2000

G   20-30

H   20-30

I   20-30

J   60-80

K   80-120

L   4000-6000

M   600-900

N   250-350

O   600-900

P 25,000-75,000

Q   800-1000

R   500-600

S   600-1000

T   20-30
Pewter
stud

U   30-40

V   40-60

W   60-100

X   40-60

Y   30-40

Z   30-40

AA   40-60

BB   40-60

CC   40-80

DD   60-125
Fob

1920 A Convict for President

In 1920 Eugene V. Debs ran for president while serving time in prison for opposing America's position in World War I. He was the candidate of the Socialist party and received nearly a million votes. His followers considered him a political prisoner. All items from his campaigns are rare and expensive.

A   400-600

B   300-500

C   400-600

D   1000-1500

E   150-200

F   250-350

G   175-275

H   40-60

I   30-60

J   3000-5000

K   40-60

L   20-40

M   40-60

N   400-600

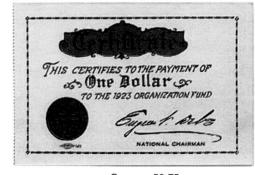

O   50-75

Woman Suffrage

Perhaps it is because women are not as apt to become collectors as men are, but for some reason, memorabilia from the campaign for woman suffrage is very rare. Some small buttons and stamps are available for under $50 but most items sell for hundreds of dollars.

A   800-1200

B   30-60

C   200-300

D   30-60
Sticker

E   30-50

F   30-50

G   30-50

H   20-40

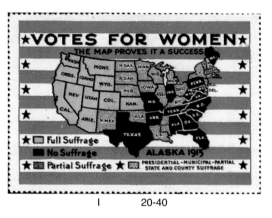

I   20-40

J   40-60

K   10-20 each
Playing card

L   200-300
Folding wax paper cup

Prohibition

Prohibition inspired numerous campaign items both pro and con. While not common, they are relatively easy to find and a nice collection can be put together in a short time.

A   15-30

B   10-20

C   3-6

D   4-8

E   4-8   Sticker

F   15-30

G   6-12

H   10-20   Post card

I   10-20

J   3-5

K   2-4

L   3-6

M   20-30

N   25-40

O   5-10   Card

P   5-8

Q   4-6

R   5-10   Window sticker

1924 Coolidge vs. Davis

John W. Davis buttons are the hardest to find of any 20th century candidate and are missing from most collections. Coolidge, having taken over after president Harding's death, was very popular and while some of his items are expensive many are easy to find.

A　300-400

B　60-85

C　150-225

D　50-75

E　60-80

F　600-800

G　300-400

H　25-40

I　30-40

J　25-40

K　6000-8000

L　1200-1800

M　2000-2500

N　4-8

O　4000-6000

P　800-1000

Q　300-325

R　1500-2000

S　125-175

T　200-300

U　40-60

V　50-75

W　900-1200

X　300-500

Y　40-60

Z　700-1200
Paper weight

1928 Hoover vs. Smith

Al Smith was the first Catholic to be nominated by a major party for president. This was an issue for some people as can be seen on buttons "M" and "N." See page 118 for another. There are some very inexpensive buttons from this election, but jugates are rare and expensive.

A   150-250

B   75-125

C   200-300

D   15-25

E   75-125

F   400-600

G   40-60

H   400-600

I   2000-3000

J   10-20

K   5-10

L   5-10

M   15-25

N   20-30

O   75-125

P   60-90

Q   40-60

R   15-25
Sticker

S   40-60

T   175-250

U   200-275

V   250-350

W   250-350

X   5-8

Y   8-12

Z   20-30

1932 Roosevelt vs. Hoover

The biggest issue of 1932 was the Great Depression and this gave Roosevelt a landslide over incumbent Herbert Hoover. There are both inexpensive, common items, and very rare items from this election.

A   200-250

B   150-200

C   30-50

D   4-8

E   10-20

F   350-450

G   75-125

H   200-250

I   200-250

J   250-350

K   15-25
Sticker

L   10-20

M   50-75

N   50-100

O   125-175

P   20-30

T   8-15

T   8-15

S   5-10

T   5-10

U   50-7   0

V   2-3

National Recovery Administration

The National Recovery Administration was one of President Roosevelt's first programs to end the depression. Under it, businesses were asked to sign a pledge to follow a business code regarding hours, prices and wages. Those which did were allowed to display the NRA Eagle emblem. Those which did not were supposed to be scorned by the populace. Some say it was modeled after the Italian corporative system under Mussolini which at the time seemed successful. The NRA ended in 1935 when it was declared unconstitutional by the Supreme Court.

L to P are stamps and stickers; Q is a pair of cloth patches on a card.

1936 Roosevelt vs. Landon

While Roosevelt's re-election in 1936 was the biggest landslide in presidential history up to that time, items for both candidates were plentiful and can range from $1 to many thousands of dollars. Both Roosevelt and Landon have many serious specialists. Because Landon was from Kansas, the symbol of his campaign was the sunflower. (It was used again in 1996 for Kansan Bob Dole.)

A   40-60

B   800-1200

C   40-60

D   4-8

E   125-175

F   5-10

G   1-2

H   1-3

I   15-20

J   3-6

K   800-1200

L   50-75

M   5-10
Sticker

N   8-15

O   200-300

P   10-15

Q   80-120

R   2-4

S   4-8

T   2-4

U   2-4

V   2-4

W   15-25
Sticker

Townsend Plan

The Townsend Plan was a proposal to provide each American over 60 with a $200 a month pension paid for by younger, working Americans. It was promoted by Francis E. Townsend, a retired physician from Long Beach, California.

A 4-8

B 2-4

C 3-6

D 2-4 Sticker

E 2-4

F 15-25

G 2-4

H 15-25

I 3-6

J 10-20

K 2-4

Father Coughlin

Father Charles Coughlin was a Catholic priest who had a radio program from 1926 to 1940. He started with mostly theological subjects and originally supported Roosevelt, but switched to economic and political subjects and eventually condemned Roosevelt. Several buttons were issued supporting him including a nine inch version.

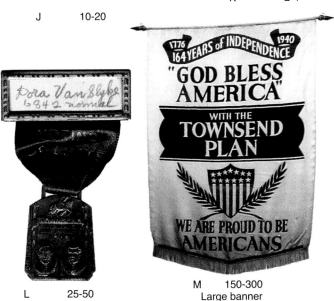

L 25-50

M 150-300
Large banner

N 25-50

1930s - 1941 Anti-War Movement

While the anti-war movement of the 1960s is well known, few realize that there was an active anti-war movement prior to our entry into World War II. With World War I just two decades past, many Americans did not want the U.S. to again get involved in a European conflict and several groups actively pushed for U.S. neutrality. But the movement died when the Japanese attacked Pearl Harbor in 1941.

A   1-2

B   1-3

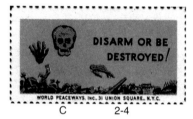

C   2-4

D   1-3

E   1-3

F   1-2

G   1-3

H   10-20

items A - G and J are stamps and stickers shown full size.

In 1939 a man in Pennsylvania had several thousand of this button made up, pinned them to the display card shown below and sold them to stores. After Pearl Harbor, he packed them away and they were forgotten until 1975 when they were discovered in the basement.

I   4-8

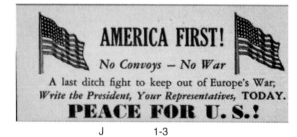

J   1-3

K   3-5
Window sticker

L   3-5
Window sticker

M   50-100

1930s and 1940s Slogan Buttons

During the 1930s and early 1940s there were hundreds of different slogan buttons produced. They were sold by street vendors holding cardboard displays at the subway stations of New York among other places, for a nickel a piece. They may have been produced primarily by Republican button makers since most of them seem to be anti-Roosevelt.

When Roosevelt's son, Elliott entered the military, he entered as a captain, whereas most American men started out as privates. This inspired a lot of different buttons.

The Third Term

Franklin Roosevelt's election in 1940 to a third term was unprecedented in U.S. history. Although Teddy Roosevelt had run for a third term on a third party and lost, even he had not served two full terms before running. Even Democrats, such as FDR's Vice President, John Nance Garner (who wanted to run for the presidency himself) and Al Smith (the 1928 Democratic nominee) opposed FDR's third term. After FDR's fourth term and death in office the U.S. Constitution was amended to limit presidents to two terms.

A   20-25   B   20-30   C   12-18   D   5-10   E   8-12

F   8-12   G   15-20   H   3-5   I   3-5   J   1-3   K   1-3

L   20-30   M   15-20   N   2-4

O   8-12   P   5-10   Q   2-4   R   30-50

1940 Roosevelt vs. Willkie

The election of 1940 was hotly contested and the Republicans thought they had a chance to regain the White House, but Roosevelt received only slightly fewer votes than in 1936 and won easily. Both Roosevelt and Willkie items are plentiful, but it is often hard to tell to which of Roosevelt's four campaigns an item belongs.

A   35-60

B   175-225

C   15-20

D   60-100

E   20-30

F   12-18

G   15-25

H   40-60

I   10-15

J   20-30

K   450-550

L   15-25

M   15-25

N   10-18

O   12-18

P   200-250

Q   100-150

R   50-85

S   80-120

T   75-100

U   3-6

V   3-6

W   40-80

X   4-7

Y   1-3

Z   1-2

AA   6-10

BB   12-20

CC   3-6

Win the War

"Win the war" items from World War II are more in the realm of militaria than political but they do represent a political cause which many collectors include in their collections.

A   100-200   B   20-30   C   50-75   D   3-6   E   20-30

F   2-4

G   3-6

H   3-6

I   1-2

J   1-3

K   1-3

L   1-3

M   1-2

N   2-4

O   1-3

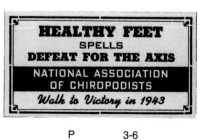

P   3-6

1944 Roosevelt vs. Dewey

If some people from both parties thought a third term was unacceptable, imagine their reaction to Roosevelt's announcement that he would seek a fourth term. He was accused of wanting a dictatorship, a royal family and worse. Some even attempted to pre-empt any future plans by sporting buttons with the slogan, "No 5th term either." While winning easily, Roosevelt died three months into his fourth term.

A   40-60

B   250-350

C   250-350

D   20-30

E   10-15

F   15-25

G   2-4

H   8-12

I   30-45

J   100-150

K   20-30

L   4-8

M   3-6

N   225-325

O   15-20

P   8-12

Q   6-10

R   1-3

S   8-12

T   10-15

U   20-30

V   20-30

1948 Truman vs. Dewey

After 16 long years out of the White House, the Republicans thought 1948 was their chance to recover it. The *Chicago Daily Tribune* was so sure of Dewey's victory that they started printing newspapers before all the results were in. That newspaper is one of the most popular and sought-after items of this election. While Dewey buttons are common, Truman buttons are the scarcest since 1924.

A   375-500

B   50-75

C   250-300

D   75-100

E   60-90

F   200-300

G   600-1200

H   200-300

I   50-75

J   60-100

K   250-350

L   25-30

M   25-30

N   30-40

O   250-350

P   40-60

Q   25-35

R   40-60

S   50-80
Heads reversed

T   10-15

U   50-75

V   40-60

W   30-50

X   20-30

Y   3-6

Z   1-3

General Douglas MacArthur

Next to Eisenhower, General MacArthur was the most sought-after candidate for president after the war. He was a hopeful for the Republican nomination in 1944, 1948 and 1952 and he was on the ballot as the presidential candidate of several small parties in the 1952 election. Not all the items issued for him were campaign pieces. Many just celebrated him as a military hero.

A   50-75

B   20-40

C   50-75
1.25 inch version

D   600-1000
9 inch version

E   6-12

F   6-12

G   20-30

H   15-30

I   6-12

J   15-30

K   75-125

L   30-40

M   6-12

N   25-35

O   10-15

P   10-15

Q   20-30

R   25-35

S   20-30

T   15-20

U   4-8

V   3-6

W   2-4

X   3-6

1952 Eisenhower vs. Stevenson

While both the Democratic and Republican parties wanted General Eisenhower to be their nominee, he decided to run as a Republican and returned the White House to the Republicans after 20 years. While there are some very rare buttons from this election there are numerous items available for about a dollar or two.

A   1-3
B   1-3
C   1-2
D   3-6
E   5-8
F   1-2

G   30-50
H   20-30
I   12-18
J   10-18
K   50-75

L   15-20
M   15-25
N1   3"   30-50
N2   1.38"   15-20
O   5-10

P   12-18
Q   12-18
R   15-25
S   15-20
T   8-12
U   2-5

V   25-40
W   20-30
X   15-25
Y   60-80

1956 Eisenhower vs. Stevenson Rematch

The Democrats decided to try a rematch of Stevenson with the incumbent Eisenhower and did even worse than in 1952. Many items clearly indicate which election they are from.

A   15-25 — AMERICA NEEDS DRAFT IKE IN 1956 DWIGHT D. EISENHOWER

B   5-8 — I STILL LIKE IKE

C   3-6 — I LIKE IKE EVEN BETTER

D   5-8 — GIVE IKE REPUBLICAN HOUSE IN '54

E   8-12 — IT   "Ike Twice"

F   25-35 — BETTER A PART-TIME PRESIDENT THAN A FULL-TIME PHONY

G   1-3 — IKE & DICK

H   1-3 — IKE AND DICK

I   10-15 — DWIGHT D. EISENHOWER

J   3-6 — STEVENSON KEFAUVER

K   3-5 — STEVENSON AND KEFAUVER

L   10-15 — ADLAI E. STEVENSON

M   6-12 — STEVENSON KEFAUVER WAGNER

N   2-4 — STEVENSON AND KEFAUVER

O   25-35 — I'M FOR STEVENSON "HOW WE'D LIKE HARRY"

P   75-100 — VOTE STRAIGHT ADLAI E. STEVENSON PRESIDENT ESTES KEFAUVER VICE PRESIDENT DEMOCRATIC TICKET

Q   25-35 — FOR '56

R   20-30 — NOW - DO YOU LIKE IKE?

1944 - 1992 Harold Stassen

Harold Stassen was a "boy wonder" who became the youngest governor of the state of Minnesota and was expected to go on to bigger and better things. His attempts to win the White House between 1940 and 1992 caused him to be labeled a perennial candidate.

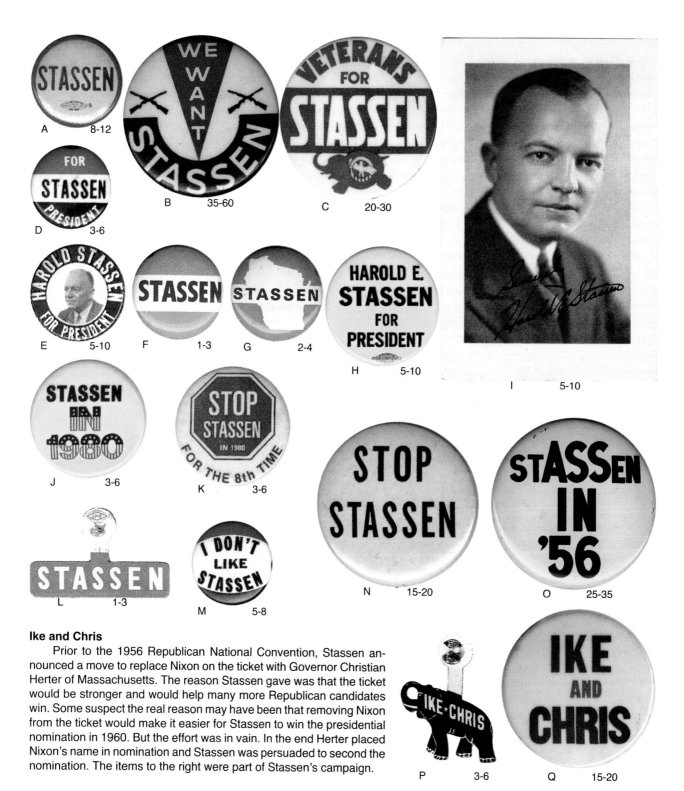

STASSEN
A   8-12

FOR STASSEN PRESIDENT
D   3-6

WE WANT STASSEN
B   35-60

VETERANS FOR STASSEN
C   20-30

HAROLD STASSEN FOR PRESIDENT
E   5-10

STASSEN
F   1-3

STASSEN
G   2-4

HAROLD E. STASSEN FOR PRESIDENT
H   5-10

I   5-10

STASSEN IN 1980
J   3-6

STOP STASSEN IN 1980 FOR THE 8th TIME
K   3-6

STASSEN
L   1-3

I DON'T LIKE STASSEN
M   5-8

STOP STASSEN
N   15-20

stASSEN IN '56
O   25-35

Ike and Chris

Prior to the 1956 Republican National Convention, Stassen announced a move to replace Nixon on the ticket with Governor Christian Herter of Massachusetts. The reason Stassen gave was that the ticket would be stronger and would help many more Republican candidates win. Some suspect the real reason may have been that removing Nixon from the ticket would make it easier for Stassen to win the presidential nomination in 1960. But the effort was in vain. In the end Herter placed Nixon's name in nomination and Stassen was persuaded to second the nomination. The items to the right were part of Stassen's campaign.

IKE·CHRIS
P   3-6

IKE AND CHRIS
Q   15-20

1960 Kennedy vs. Nixon

Because of President Kennedy's assassination, his items are among the most popular of recent presidents. While some are common, the best ones command prices of many thousands of dollars.

A   3-6

B   15-20
Dark blue bottom

C   15-20

D   5-10

E   5-10

F   2-4

G   40-80

H   7-15

I   8-12

J   25-40

K   10,000-15,000

L   5-10

M   15-25

N   8-12

O   1-2

P   1-2

Q   1-2

R   8-12

S   5-8

T   3-6

U   8-12

V   4-8

W   5-10

X   8-12

Y   10-15

Z   15-25

1964 Johnson vs. Goldwater

While Goldwater's conservatism attracted some fervent followers, President Johnson's continuation of the martyred President Kennedy's programs helped him win a landslide victory in 1964.

A   2-4 — AFL-CIO COPE FOR LBJ & HHH

B   1-2 — LBJ FOR THE USA

C   1-2 — ELECT JOHNSON AND HUMPHREY VOTE DEMOCRATIC

D   1-2 — JOHNSON HUMPHREY

E   5-8 — L.B.J.

F   6-12 — BURY BARRY

G   8-12 — "LET US CONTINUE..." JOHNSON – HUMPHREY

H   4-8 — JOHNSON AND HUMPHREY

I   1-2 — ALL THE WAY WITH LBJ

J   8-12 — Lyndon Baker Jenkins — Anti-Johnson

K   1-2 — JOHNSON AND HUMPHREY

L   8-12 — GOLDWATER In '64

M   20-30 — PENINSULA CITIZENS FOR GOLDWATER

N   4-8 — GOLDWATER FOR PRESIDENT

O   20-25 — PA. YOUTH FOR GOLDWATER

P   2-4 — GOLDWATER IN '64

Q   5-10

R   8-12 — H₂O

S   1-2 — GOLDWATER MILLER 64

T   1-2 — GOLDWATER AND MILLER

U   4-8 — BARRY GOLDWATER FOR PRESIDENT

V   8-12

W   8-12

X   10-15 — I.Y.H. Y.K. H.R.

Y   6-12 — A CHOICE NOT AN ECHO GOLDWATER – MILLER

Z   15-20 — I AM A RIGHT-WING "EXTREMIST"

AA   75-100 — EXTREMISM IN THE DEFENSE OF LIBERTY IS NO VICE; MODERATION IN THE PURSUIT OF JUSTICE IS NO VIRTUE GOLDWATER IN '64

Communism and Anti-Communism

Today we can look back on communism as a seventy-year experiment in tyranny, but during that time many Americans felt our country was in a life or death struggle with a powerful foe. Once the secret files were opened after the fall of the Soviet Union, it was interesting to see which side was right in many of the hottest American political debates of the 1950s and 1960s.

A   3-6

B   2-4

C   1-2

D   1-2

E   1-2

F   25¢-50¢

G   1-2

H   2-4

I   1-3

J   50¢-1

K   1-2

L   1-3

M   10-20

N   20-30

O   50-75

P   15-25

Q   3-6

R   20-40

S   10-20

T   20-30

U   15-25

V   10-20

W   12-25

Vietnam War

The Vietnam War was one of the most divisive times in American history. There are many political items from that era, most of which opposed the war.

A   1-3

B   2-4

C   8-15

D   1-3

E   5-10
We Don't Want
Your F-------- War

F   40-60

G   2-4

H   3-6

I   4-8

J   2-4

K   4-8
Lamppost sticker

L   4-8
Lamppost sticker

M   4-8
Lamppost sticker

N   2-3
Bumper sticker

O   2-4
Bumper sticker

P   1-3
Window sticker

Q   2-4
Bumper sticker

1968 Nixon vs. Humphrey and Wallace

Many of today's collectors of political items started in the exciting campaign of 1968. That year produced a surge of collector-made buttons and a three-way race that changed the party in the White House. Today the items sell for from less than a dollar to up to hundreds of dollars each.

A   2-4

B   50¢-1

C   50¢-1

D   50¢-1

E   1-2

F   5-8

G   1-3

H   6-10

I   50¢-1

J   1-2

K   1-2

L   10-20

M   10-15

N   3-6

O   4-8

P   4-8

Q   6-12

R   4-8

S   4-8

T   4-8

U   6-12

V   4-8

W   4-8

X   4-8

Y   5-10

FOR PRESIDENT HUBERT H. HUMPHREY

A   3-6

HHH FILLS THE PRESCRIPTION

B   12-15

HUBIE BABY

C   4-8

Humphrey for PRESIDENT

D   2-5

HUMPHREY MUSKIE

E   4-8

HUMPHREY-MUSKIE VOTE DEMOCRAT

F   3-6

HUMPHREY MUSKIE

G   1-2

HHH

H   1-2

HHH Humphrey

I   1-2

Wallace for PRESIDENT STAND UP FOR AMERICA

J   50¢-1

WALLACE LeMAY

K   50¢-1

Wallace FOR PRESIDENT

L   50¢-1

WALLACE FOR PRESIDENT

M   3-5

HUMPHREY ★★★ MUSKIE

N   50¢-1

FOR PRESIDENT GEORGE WALLACE

O   2-5

WALLACE for PRESIDENT STAND UP FOR AMERICA

P   1-2

Tweedle Dee ☐ Tweedle Dum ☐ WALLACE ☒

Q   4-6

HOME • HELP HUSTLE HUBERT 4-H CLUB

R   4-6

S   10-15

WALLACE LeMAY

T   4-8

WALLACE FOR PRESIDENT

U   2-4

V   5-8

Pro-Choice vs. Pro-Life

The abortion issue is still with us today, but in the 1970s it was an especially hot issue with people from around the country marching in Washington and other cities several times a year. Hundreds of buttons were issued during this time and they can still be found at very reasonable prices. One-day event buttons are of course much scarcer than buttons sold regularly over the years.

1972 Nixon vs. McGovern

In 1972 President Nixon won the biggest landslide since 1936, only to resign two years later over the Watergate affair. In quantity, common buttons from 1972 can cost as little as 10¢ each, but the better ones can cost hundreds of dollars.

A   3-6

B   3-6

C   1-2

D   2-4

E   50¢-1

F   50¢-1

G   50¢-1

H   50¢-1

I   2-4

J   3-5

K   50¢-1

L   50¢-1

M   2-4

N   4-8

O   50¢-1

P   50-100

Q   25-50

R   150-250

S   1-3

T   5-8

U   100-150

V   100-150

W   6-12

X   300-400

Watergate

The break-in at the Democratic Party Headquarters by Republican operatives, ending in the first resignation of a sitting president inspired in many interesting items for both sides which can still be found at very reasonable prices.

A   3-8   B   3-8   C   3-8   D   3-8   E   3-8   F   3-8

G   3-8   H   3-8   I   3-8   J   3-8   K   3-8

L   3-5   M   3-8   N   3-8   O   3-8   P   10-15

Q   1-2   R   15-20   S   1-2   T   1-2

U   2-4
The Nation magazine opposed Nixon

V   8-12
Reference to Teddy Kennedy

Whip Inflation Now

In response to one of the biggest crises of the 1970s, inflation, President Ford initiated a program called "Whip Inflation Now" or WIN. Hundreds of varieties of buttons were issued to promote the program, many by private businesses. They are relatively inexpensive and most Ford collectors include these items in their collections. There were several satirical versions made, two of which are shown here.

A   1-2   B   1-2   C   1-2   D   3-6   E   3-6   F   3-6   G   2-4   H   1-2

I   8-12   J   4-8   K   8-12   L   3-6

M   6-10   N   6-10

O   8-12
Flasher

P   3-6

Q   10-20

1976 Carter vs. Ford

After the Watergate scandal, Americans were not so excited by politics. There was not even a World's Fair for the Bicentennial in 1976. Fewer political items were made in 1976 than in 1972 and Gerald Ford, who had replaced both Vice-President Agnew and President Nixon was turned out of the White House for the fresh ideas of the peanut farmer from Georgia, Jimmy Carter. Ford items are scarcer than most other candidates of the era, but there are some inexpensive items available for both candidates.

A   50¢-1   B   3-6   C   3-6   D   10-15   E   5-8   F   6-10

G   15-20   H   20-40   I   4-8   J   10-15

K   3-6   L   5-10   M   3-5   N   50¢-1   O   50¢-1   P   150-250

Q   3-6   R   3-6 Button made from sticker   S   200-300   T   250-350

1980 Reagan vs. Carter and Anderson

On July 15, 1979 President Carter gave what some consider the most important speech of his presidency, which became known as the malaise speech. Americans agreed with him and in 1980 replaced him with Ronald Reagan who promised to "make America great again." John Anderson, a liberal Republican congressman from Illinois started his own party to run against Carter and Reagan, but he didn't attract much support. Items from this election range from less than a dollar to hundreds of dollars.

A   4-8   B   4-8   C   4-8   D   3-6   E   1-2   F   1-2   G   1-2

H   20-30   I   20-40   J   10-20   K   20-30

L   50¢-1   M   4-8   N   3-6   O   3-6   P   1-2

Q   4-6   R   8-12   S   2-4   T   4-8

1984 Reagan vs. Mondale

While President Reagan was reviled by the left, mainstream America loved his positive outlook and he was re-elected in 1984 with the electoral votes of a record 49 states. Mondale's choice of the first female running mate of a major party was historic, but did not help him in the election.

A   6-12   B   2-4   C   2-4   D   50¢-1   E   3-5

F   20-30   G   8-12   H   8-12   I   5-8

J   50¢-1   K   50¢-1   L   3-6   M   5-8   N   3-6

O   3-5   P   3-6   Q   6-12   R   3-6

1988 Bush vs. Dukakis

While Michael Dukakis easily outshined his Democratic rivals, he was no match for Reagan's Vice President, George H. W. Bush. Most Dukakis and Bush items are inexpensive and overlooked by many collectors.

A   5-10

B   5-8

C   3-6

D   3-5

E   5-8

F   5-8

G   5-8

H   3-5

I   100-300

J   5-8

K   6-12

L   6-12

M   25-50

N1   3-6
N2   Without UAW seal 1-3

O   50¢-1

P   2-4

Gulf War

The Gulf War to liberate Kuwait from the Iraqi invasion inspired many political items on both sides, but at present there is little demand for them and they are available very cheaply. There were at least 6 different sets of trading cards produced. Cards picturing President Bush, Secretary of Defense Cheney and the generals are the most desirable. Those picturing ships or planes least. If Cheney or Powell becomes president their cards should be worth more.

| A | 2-4 | B | 1-2 | C | 2-4 | D | 2-5 | E | 2-5 |

| F | 1-2 | G | 2-4 | H | 3-6 | I | 2-4 |

| J | 2-5 | K | 2-4 | L | 2-4 | M | 2-4 |

| N | 3-6 |
| Silk-screened on wood pinback | |

| O | 2-5 | P | 2-5 | Q | 1-2 |

1992 Clinton vs. Bush and Perot

H. Ross Perot, whose buttons are shown on the next page, may have tipped the 1992 election to Bill Clinton, who won with just 43% of the vote. But Clinton and his wife Hillary have inspired strong feelings on both sides of the political spectrum. While George H. W. Bush items are not in great demand, classic Clinton items get very high prices.

A   200-400
Hillary Clinton asked that
this button be taken off
the market.

B   3-5

C   3-5

D   8-15

E   3-6

F   5-10

G   3-8

H   3-5

I   8-15

J   4-8

K   3-5

L   5-10

M   5-10

N   6-10

O   3-6

P   50¢-1

Q   3-6

R   4-8

H. Ross Perot

When H. Ross Perot entered the presidential race in 1992 it generated political excitement not seen since at least 1968. All over the country people opened offices to support his candidacy. But when he withdrew, and then re-entered the campaign, he lost credibility and finished third, but with the best third party showing since Teddy Roosevelt in 1912. Finding every button issued by every group supporting Perot would be a real challenge.

A   10-20

B   4-8

C   3-6

D   3-5

E   3-5

F   3-6

G   5-8
Electric light

H   4-8

I   5-10

J   3-6

K   50¢-1

L   10-20

M   5-10
Actual currency used

N   3-6

O   2-4

P   2-4

1996 Clinton vs. Dole

The 1996 election was one of the least exciting in recent memory. Sitting presidents are hard to beat, and Bob Dole offered the least excitement one could hope for in the campaign. Dole items are uniformly overlooked while some Clinton items are very desirable.

A   3-5

B   3-6

C   100-300

D   1-2

E   10-20
Aretha Franklin gave a concert during the
1996 Democratic National Convention

F   3-5

G   1-2

H   50¢-1

I   3-5

J   3-6

K   5-10
Glows in dark

L   3-5

M   2-4

N   3-5

O   5-10

P   3-6

2000 Bush vs. Gore

While the 2000 election offered the excitement of a change of president no matter who won, no one expected the kind of excitement this election resulted in. For the best buttons of this election see the next page.

A   2-4

B   3-6

C   2-4

D   4-8

E   3-6

F   3-6

G   3-6

H   50¢-1

I   2-4

J   2-4

K   50¢-1

L   1-3

M   3-5

N   2-4

O   3-6

P   2-4

Q   3-5

R   3-5

2000 Election Crisis

When the election night vote count turned out to be a virtual dead heat for Florida's deciding electoral votes, the country began a five-week wait to find out its next president. During this time both sides of the controversy put out buttons.

A   2-5

B   2-5

C   3-5

D   2-5

E   3-5

F   3-5

G   3-5

H   2-4

I   2-5

J   2-5

K   15-25
Press Credential

L   3-6

M   2-5

N   2-4
Sticker

September 11, 2001

While most businesses were loathe to appear to capitalize on the tragedy of September 11th, many people wanted some remembrance or expression of their feelings from that day. These buttons were some of those released for that tragedy.

2004 Bush vs. Kerry

With the Internet allowing more sellers to reach more buyers, it appears that the number of different buttons for the 2004 election may reach an all time record. When deciding which buttons you should save from this election, you should look for nice artwork combined with a clever slogan, or a theme especially unique to this campaign.

A   2-5

B   2-4

C   2-4

D   2-4

E   2-4

F   4-8

G   2-4

H   4-8

I   2-4

J   4-8

K   2-5

L   5-35

M   2-4

N   50¢-1

O   50¢-1

A   8-12

B   2-5

C   2-5

D   2-3

E   2-3

H   1-2

I   2-3

J   2-3

F   1-2

G   1-2

K   2-4
For John Kerry Before Iowa

L   2-5

M   2-4

N   4-6

O   5-10

P   2-4

Q   1-2

Part II - Collecting Political Campaign Items

Where to Find Political Campaign Items

The Internet

When the last edition of this book was published, the best place to find political items was at political collectibles shows (see below) but today the Internet is by far the best. In fact this may be the golden age of putting together a collection because so many items are coming out of attics, basements and jewel boxes and being offered for the first time since they were made.

Imagine, a few years ago if you collected, say, Nixon items you could go to every antique store and collectibles shop in your city and you'd find, maybe, a few common buttons which were always overpriced. Today you can type in "Nixon" in eBay's search engine and find at least 500 items.

While people may have been afraid they would not get a fair price for grandma's old buttons at their local antique shop, today they can be sure that hundreds if not thousands of serious collectors from around the globe will get to bid on them and they will get the highest price anyone would bid.

The Internet is still relatively new, and many people don't know how easy it is to sell things, so it will probably be a goldmine for decades to come. Recently businesses have opened that help people sell their things on-line. So older people who do not have computers will be able to sell their things on-line.

As explained in the chapter on pricing, the Internet will not only let sellers get record prices for their items, it will also help buyers get items at better prices.

Right now eBay is by far the best place for finding political items. Some sellers who have gotten made at eBay have gone to other on-line auctions, or started their own sites, but none of these have been anywhere near as good as eBay. Unless eBay really abuses its position, it will probably continue to be the best source on-line.

Most political items on eBay are under Collectibles>Historical>Political, and many political buttons can also be found under Collectibles>Pinbacks, Nodders, Lunchboxes>Pinbacks>Political. But political items like sheet music, stamps, glassware, and other items can be found in other categories.

The best way to get a good deal is to find an item in a category where most political collectors wouldn't look, or to find an item that is not well described. The author once won a John W. Davis picture button for $20 because it was listed with a lot of calendars that were listed under seed advertising items. But such luck only comes with tedious searching. When a seller titles his lot "political buttons" you can hope there will be a rare button that no one else noticed, but it's not likely.

Auctions

There are several political auctions that offer more good items in one catalog than eBay has in a whole year. If you are looking for older and better items, and want to build your collection quickly, you should subscribe to some of these auctions. They are not cheap, but most of them list all prices realized, so you can learn the value of items you are looking for.

It used to be that political auction prices were a lot higher than prices at political shows. But recently more collectors are putting their good items in auctions. So many items you will probably never find for sale except at auctions.

Auction fever can be a problem for rare items. Often key items will go for double or triple their estimated value, if two or more bidders "must have" the item to complete their collection and do not want to wait five years for another to surface. Occasionally the same item will be in another auction six months later and cost only half its previous high because only one serious collector is left who needs it.

But there will also be bargains at auctions. With hundreds or thousands of items to choose from, many items which appear regularly in the auctions do not get any bids, and can be picked up reasonably. Don't expect to steal the items. If the only bid on a $200 item is $35 the auctioneer or consignor will either withdraw the item or bid himself. But some items can be bought for 80 or even 60 percent of the estimate.

The larger political shows usually have one or two auctions. One usually consists of items consigned by the members. Many rare and unusual items appear at these auctions and often the prices are very reasonable.

A list of political auctioneers is included in Appendix 1.

Political Collectibles Shows

A few years ago the best place to find a good selection of political items at a fair price was from other collectors at political collectibles shows. These are held all over the country throughout the year and offer an unbelievable variety of all types of items. Smaller shows might have 10 or 20 tables but regional and national shows have 100 to 300 tables. Nearly all of the dealers and collectors at the events have scoured their area for political items to bring to these shows. Sometimes collectors decide to sell their collections and come to a show to dispose of it. If they have not collected for a while they may not realize the current prices and may offer bargains.

The Internet seems to have lessened the attendance at these shows in recent years. Some believe that a few hours on-line can provide as many items as a trip to a show. But the shows are a great way to compare prices and to get a lot of items at one time. The larger shows have auctions which feature rare items that come available very seldom.

While it takes time and money to travel to these shows, it can be well worth it for the serious collector. Some collectors take time off work and fly across the country to attend these shows because the opportunity is so great to obtain good items at a fair price. Often a few bargains can more than pay for all of your expenses. Knowledgeable collectors have been able to buy, sell and trade items at the same show and make enough profit to pay for the trip.

Lists of upcoming political shows are published in the publications *Political Bandwagon* and *Political Collector*.

Price Lists and Ads by Collectors

Some collectors of political items finance their collection by dealing in political items. If their local antique dealer has three identical Kennedy buttons, they don't buy just one for their collection, they get all three and sell the extras. Since prices are so fluid, it is easy to make a profit on items you buy, either immediately, or a few years later.

Today, price lists are used by collectors more for new buttons, since they are selling their older ones on eBay. But some collectors still have lists. Display ads in the political collectibles newspapers (see Appendix 1 for names and addresses) picture numerous items for sale, and classified ads offer photocopied lists of hundreds of items.

Antique Stores and Flea Markets

Local antique stores can offer both the best deals and the worst deals in political items. Because of the lack of knowledge of most dealers they often price items by their "gut feeling." This may mean an old button, a colorful one, or one for a popular figure has a high price and a new button, an ugly one, or one for someone they have never heard of is priced low. Because of this, a dealer may have a common

Nixon button (which is worth 50¢), and a rare Davis button (worth $500) both priced at $10.

One danger of buying at antique stores and flea markets is fakes. While attendees of political shows are forbidden from selling such items, no such rules apply to others. Until you become knowledgeable about political items be careful about buying expensive items from antique and flea market dealers. More information on fakes is included in a later chapter.

Many antique and flea market dealers are starting to discover the political item reference catalogs on the market and this can be either good or bad for the collector. It can eliminate the great bargains, but also the overpricing. Because some items have risen in price rapidly, the prices even in recent catalogs may be low. But most dealers ignore the comments in the catalogs about condition and think their badly damaged items are still worth the figure in the catalog which applies to an item in good condition.

Advertising

Many collectors have luck advertising to buy items in local newspapers, shoppers, antique publications and various collectibles publications. Those with special interests often advertise in the political collectors' newspapers. The author has had some luck advertising in the hometown newspaper of various candidates, and in towns where special events took place and one-day buttons were issued.

Political Headquarters

The days are gone when you could walk into a political campaign headquarters and grab a handful of buttons out of a bowl. Buttons are expensive and the money is believed to be better spent on television spots. For rallies, some candidates even substitute paper stickers for buttons (see page 134). Some candidates sell their buttons or only give them to donors. Many headquarters have no buttons at all.

But don't neglect stopping in your local headquarters, you might get lucky. Some local groups create their own buttons and you may end up with the only ones in the hobby.

Occasionally special buttons will be issued for staff members, volunteers or contributors. Sometimes these are also given away freely, other times the staff guards them with their lives. You should ask if there are any special limited-edition buttons. If you bring along some other colorful buttons for the candidate, or even earlier inexpensive Kennedy or Reagan buttons you might be able to trade for a rare staff button. Some collectors even volunteer to work on the campaign in order to get a rare button.

Some people have luck writing to campaign headquarters. Including a stamped, self-addressed (padded) envelope might increase your chances, but if they don't have any buttons you will have wasted your postage. Some collectors invest in a phone call to important headquarters to ask what is available.

Keep in mind that there are headquarters for specific candidates, for groups supporting certain candidates, and for the party organizations. Any of these might have unusual or rare buttons.

The Federal Election Commission (FEC) has the addresses of all candidates' headquarters available as public records. Many collectors have requested the list and had good luck writing to the addresses listed. The FEC web site is at www.fec.gov.

More helpful than the FEC web site is Ron Gunzberger's Politics1.com web site. Ron has links to the web sites of every party and nearly every candidate for every office. Some of his useful pages are:
2004 Presidential Race: www.politics1.com/p2004.htm
Third Parties: www.politics1.com/parties.htm
State Candidates: www.politics1.com/states.htm

Fairs and Marches

During an election year, state and county fairs usually have booths for political candidates. These are often stocked with buttons and sometimes have locally-produced buttons not available elsewhere. Political marches and rallies often attract vendors who sell buttons. Sometimes these are one-day dated buttons that can turn out to be rare.

Political Conventions

Political conventions can be one of the best places to get buttons and other campaign memorabilia. Collectors attending these events have brought home bags and boxes of thousands of items which last for years of future trading.

At political conventions you can find items put out by political organizations and by numerous vendors. At the national conventions many state delegations put out their own buttons, and every street corner around the convention site may have vendors selling buttons. At recent national conventions there have been huge halls just for vendors to sell all types of political souvenirs. Keep in mind that besides the Democratic and Republican National Conventions, there are third party national conventions and state and local political conventions.

Many rare and limited edition buttons can be found at conventions and many collectors spend a week at both of the major party national nominating conventions. A key way to get good buttons is to trade for them. Delegates who were given boring-looking, but rare, buttons for their delegation often will trade them for a more colorful or older button.

2004 Candidate Web Sites

Just as television once revolutionized campaigning, many feel the internet will soon do the same. Most candidates in the current race for the White House and many local political groups have web sites. These sites typically give the position of the candidate on the issues, a list of those who have endorsed the candidate, and some even include instructions for ordering buttons and other campaign items.

The following are some sites which were current at the time of publication of this book:

Republican Party
http://www.georgewbush.com/

Democratic Party
http://www.johnkerry.com/

American Party
http://www.theamericanparty.org/

Constitution Party
http://www.constitution-party.net/
http://www.peroutka2004.com/

Green Party
http://www.gp.org/

Libertarian Party
http://www.lp.org/

Ralph Nader
http://www.votenader.org/

Natural Law Party
http://www.natural-law.org/

Peace & Freedom Party
http://www.peaceandfreedom.org/

Prohibition Party
http://www.prohibition.org/

Reform Party
http://www.reformparty.org

Socialist Party
http://www.sp-usa.org/

Socialist Equality Party
http://www.socialequality.com/
http://www.wsws.org/articles/2004/jan2004/stat-j27.shtml

Socialist Workers Party
http://www.themilitant.com/

Other Candidates
http://www.allan2004.com/
http://www.joebellis.com/
http://members.aol.com/johng101/jonpol.htm
http://www.ufu.gq.nu/
http://www.angelfire.com/ga4/g_hough/index.html
http://www.darrenforpresident.com/
http://www.joeforpresident.org/
http://www.muadin.com/
http://www.wethepeople-wtp.org/
http://www.voteforjoe.com/
http://www.dansnow2004.com/
http://lrtopham.tripod.com/
http://www.lightparty.com/Write-In.html

Vendor vs. "Official" Items

Since the 1960s there has been a debate within the hobby concerning the relative value of "official" versus "vendor" campaign items. There is a small group of collectors which feels that the only political items worth collecting are so-called

"official" items. These collectors shun anything that was made by a commercial vendor for sale to the public, and especially items made by collectors. They feel so strongly about their position that they would expel anyone who made buttons from the collectors' organization, APIC.

The problem with this position is the most beautiful (and valuable) items ever made were vendor items, and the arguments against them are spurious.

What are Vendor Items?

Vendor items are political items designed and manufactured by a private company to sell to the general public and to campaign organizations. The first vendor campaign items were produced for the 1840 election and they have been made ever since then. We can find

catalogs and ads in newspapers for nearly every campaign showing numerous campaign items offered by private vendors. One catalog was distributed by the Republican party in 1956 listing private vendors of various items available to its local chapters. Even when ads cannot be found, when campaign items are found in matched sets we can see that they were not designed by one party, but by an independent vendor for sale to both parties.

The Abraham Lincoln photo pins, the beautiful multicolored buttons of the "Golden Age" of buttons, nearly all jugates, and the most creative buttons of nearly every campaign were all "unofficial" and sold by private vendors for a profit.

What are "Official" Items?

"Official" buttons, on the other hand, are those conceived and/or authorized by some campaign committee or support group. They are often plain, colorless and sometimes ugly. But the collector of "official" buttons finds more joy in obtaining a small two-color button from a small labor union than a clever multi-colored cartoon button produced by a vendor.

A good example of an official button is the "Nixon Now" litho button from 1972. These were made by the millions and given away freely by Nixon's re-election committee. Most collectors have a bag full and there are enough around for every collector who will ever be born.

The Obsession of Completeness

Why do some collectors shun "unofficial buttons"? Partly for financial reasons. Some vendor items are made in limited quantities and sold at ridiculous prices. For many collectors, completeness becomes not just a goal, but an obsession. Part of the fun of collecting is working toward the goal of a complete collection, and getting a little closer to that goal every few weeks or months keeps the hobby exciting.

If anyone can make a single political button and price it at, say, $100, the obsessed collector is at their mercy. Either he gets ripped off, or his collection will *never be complete*. Completeness is so important to some collectors that the proliferation of vendor buttons has caused them to give up collecting modern buttons.

Collector-Made Buttons

At some point in the evolution of the hobby of political button collecting, some collector realized that if he had a button designed and manufactured, he would be able to trade those buttons for buttons he needed for his collection. Eventually he realized that since he was the only source for that button, he could ask whatever he wanted and those collectors obsessed with completeness would have to pay his price.

This caused an uproar in the hobby. Collectors realized that if every collector could make his own button and ask ridiculous prices it would be hard for anyone to have a complete collection. And what if some collectors made only one or two copies of a button? Those would then be the rarest buttons in the hobby. Some predicted that this would cause the total collapse of the hobby, since no one could have a *complete collection*.

To avoid this catastrophe strict ethical rules were promulgated by the APIC. No collector was allowed to create political buttons unless he was part of an official campaign organization and then he had to disclose his affiliation and could only keep one-half of 1% of the buttons.

Yet collectors still made buttons. In the 1950s and 1960s two popular areas of collecting were jugates and third party buttons. But the small parties were not producing these buttons. Who do you think made all the jugates for such obscure parties as the Greenback Party and the Vegetarian Party? Members, or friends of members, of APIC.

Collector-made buttons really blossomed in 1968. That year, due to the youth movement for Eugene McCarthy and the general political excitement of the time, many more people started collecting political buttons. As usual the parties produced dull and boring buttons. At the Nixon headquarters you could get red and white "Nixon's the One!" buttons in three (small) sizes.

But the vendors of the day filled the need with hundreds of buttons in all sizes, colors and shapes. These were sold at very reasonable prices and were available in adequate quantities for all who wanted them.

Still the "purists" in the hobby complained that these buttons were "unofficial" and "junk" and would ruin the hobby. At least one manufacturer, some of whose buttons are now classics, was expelled from APIC. Other manufacturers, who had been in the button business for many years, were told they could not join the APIC. Every person on the planet could make a political button except a member of

APIC. All button dealers who were APIC members were asked to sign an affidavit, but to the disappointment of the officers, their lawyers pointed out that it would violate anti-trust laws.

Shortly after the 1968 election things did somewhat get out of hand. In designing buttons for 1972, manufacturers realized that one design could be printed in 5 or more colors of ink and that at least 10 colors of paper were available. This meant that a single piece of artwork could result in 50 different buttons, including such garish and unreadable combinations as green on yellow and red on dark green.

As America's interest in politics declined after Watergate, so did the frenzy of collector-made buttons. It did not pick up again until 1992 when Americans again were excited by the prospect of a serious third party candidate and Democrats were excited by the first chance in years of regaining the White House. In this excitement many APIC members began making buttons. By November, 1992 it was joked at an APIC convention that the new rule was that a member would be expelled if he *didn't* produce a button.

While many members felt that it didn't matter who made buttons, a majority of the board of directors still wanted to limit what members could make. A new ethics rule was approved in 1995 which forbids members from making items "primarily to sell or trade to collectors."

Should You Collect "Vendor" Buttons?

Today few collectors try to obtain every button, there are just too many. What most do is collect a representative sample of each candidate. Even those who specialize in a single candidate feel free to pass on overpriced items without obsessing over completeness.

The fact is, the best items from most campaigns have nearly all been vendor buttons and 20 years after an election is over few people care. They want the most interesting and attractive buttons from the campaign. Vendor buttons which were shunned at 25¢ during the campaign have passed the $100 mark years later.

The best answer is to collect what you like and find attractive, and buttons that give some special insight to the issues of the campaign. Most vendor buttons are priced very reasonably, and some will be classics some day.

If you see someone asking $25 or $100 for a button for the current election, be wary. It might be a classic some day, but there might be 499 more of them put away for the manufacturer's children's college fund.

It is believed that all buttons pictured in this chapter are vendor buttons except the "Nixon Now" button.

How Much to Pay for Items

There is an old saying among political collectors that you don't have to worry if you overpaid for an item because it will eventually be worth whatever you paid. Still, most collectors seek to find the best deals and buy as many items with the money they have available.

Values

The values of political items are not as fixed as those of other collectibles such as stamps and coins. This is because the quantities made of most political items is unknown and the collector demand is not as deep as for some other collectibles. Also, until recently there has not been a simple way for buyers and sellers to find each other, but the Internet has changed all that.

With stamps and coins the printings and mintages are known precisely, and prices are tracked annually and even weekly by catalogs and newsletters. With political items, not all items are known, quantities made are unknown, some items come up for sale only once every several years, and every year new items are discovered that have never before been known.

This situation helps make the hobby more exciting. It is not unusual to sell an item for double, triple, or even ten times what you paid for it once you become knowledgeable. It is not unusual for a dealer at a political collectibles show to buy an item from another dealer and sell it to another person at the same show for double or triple what he paid.

But this volatility also adds some risk. If you don't pay attention to prices you can easily pay double or triple what an item is worth at the time.

As explained at the beginning of this book, the prices given in this book are in ranges. Some of these ranges are wide. But the reality of the market is that prices do vary that much and more. Because there are a lot of collectors looking for bargains, items usually won't sell for below the range given in this book. But if two determined collectors are after the same item it can sell for well above the range.

The flexibility of prices offers a lot of opportunity for building a valuable collection at a reasonable price. If you follow the political auctions and watch the prices you can find lots of bargains. In smaller auctions, the auctioneer usually has a reserve on an item and won't allow anything to go too cheaply. But in the larger auctions there are almost always some items selling well below their fair value. The auctioneer figures that since some items sell for well above their expected value, some can go for bargain prices and the auction will be a success and some bidders will be extra happy.

The most important thing is to watch prices for a while and learn the market. If you are serious about building a collection, you should subscribe to at least two political auctions. The names and addresses are listed in Appendix 1, and if you never subscribed they will probably give you a free first copy. Most auctions give you the prices realized either in the next issue or on a separate sheet.

These will help you see what items are available and what you can expect to pay. The prices realized will help you learn if an item is selling within its estimate or rising or falling.

Buying

The most economical way to build a collection is to be flexible. If you have to have a certain item for your collection, you will need to bid against all the others looking for that item. If you have a wide range of items you are looking for, you can buy only the ones that no one else is bidding on.

When you bid in an auction, usually you get an item for just one bid, or perhaps 10% above the next bidder. This may lead you to believe that whatever you bid, you can't overpay more than 10% over what the item is worth. This is not true. While most collectors watch the market and make reasonable bids, there are always a few collectors who don't care if they overpay. A collector who wants to quickly build a great collection and has a large budget, one who has looked for an item for many years, one who needs just this item to complete a set, may all pay well over market value for an item in an auction. Also, if someone wants an item for a gift, price may not be important.

So you need to have some sense of value before bidding in an auction. If an item very rarely comes available then paying well above its estimate may be wise. But some expensive items come to auction a couple times a year, so it is not wise to bid one up over its normal value just because another collector wants it very badly too. Rather than fight him for it and paying 50% more than its worth, let him have this one and buy it next time when he won't be bidding.

This strategy usually works, but not always. In the 1980s Abraham Lincoln ferrotypes were regularly selling for about $100 each. They are not rare so each political auctioneer had several available in his auctions each year. If you were willing to pay a little extra, say $125 or $135 you could easily win them. But then in the late 1980s some baseball card collectors got interested in political items. The Lincoln ferrotypes seemed like a steal at $100, so they began to bid them up to $300 and even $500. Since then the price has stayed at those levels and never settled back down.

Hot items

Be careful of "hot" or "limited edition" items issued during a campaign. For example during President Carter's campaign some buttons came out which were thought to be very rare and collectors bid them up to several hundred dollars. But a few years later it became apparent that there were plenty of the buttons available and the price dropped significantly. Today they still sell for well under a hundred dollars.

Sometimes during a campaign you see an expensive item that looks like it may be a classic and you want to buy it before it gets even more expensive. But you should realize that it could also be available much cheaper. On eBay, many buttons from the current campaign are bid up to $25, $50, even $100, but the same buttons are available from the manufacturers on their web sites for under $2!

Buttons put out by labor unions or other small groups might be good ones to pay a bit extra for, but not always. Some button manufacturers offer to make buttons for small groups, but then also sell them to their collector customers. In fact some may sell more to collectors than to the groups.

Defective Items

One important factor to keep in mind is that most prices quoted for buttons are for those in sound condition. A crack or a stain on a button can make it worth only 1/10th or 1/20th of the value of a mint item. Fading, separation of the celluloid from the paper or rim, rust, and scratches all lessen the value of a button. Tears, holes and adhesive tape stains lower the value of paper and cloth items.

However, when an item is very rare or unique, such as a Lincoln flag or Polk bandanna, damage would not detract as much from the value because there just isn't another available.

Investing

In many hobbies people who collect with an eye on making a profit on their collection are looked down upon by those who claim to collect purely from a love of the items, and this is also somewhat true of political collectors. Collectors who love the items are angry that they have to pay more and more to build their collections.

But the reality is that few people would pay $5,000 or $1,000 or even $100 on a collectible that they expect to be worthless some day. When you pay that much for a political item you expect that you'll be able to sell it for at least what you paid.

Recent comments in collectible publications indicate that the reason for the rise in popularity of baseball cards over coins was the excitement of the possibility of receiving a rare card in a pack. It may be part of the lottery mentality, or perhaps collectors are all misers at heart, but the possibility of quick or steady profit is something that excites most collectors.

Happily, unless you ridiculously overpay for political items, you will eventually at least get your money back and in most cases make a handsome profit. One political collector, who is a stock broker, sometimes shows his clients how much more they could have made if they had bought political buttons instead of stocks.

As the ads say, "past performance is no guaranty of future results." But, except for some temporary dips in the market, political campaign items have steadily risen in value, year after year. With supplies of good items limited to begin with, prices rise almost yearly as new collectors enter the hobby. Some buttons which sold for $25 and $50 twenty years ago sell for $500 to $1200 today. A price list from a decade ago has prices one-half to one-quarter what they are today.

Some of the best buttons are only known to exist in quantities of a few dozen. If a few wealthy new collectors start bidding in auctions, they could cause the value of those pins to quickly double or triple. But if several old-time collectors decide it is time to sell, or if a handful is discovered in an attic, the price could suddenly drop.

Fortunately for those who consider their collection an investment, such drops are seldom and are usually short term. Discoveries of rare buttons tend to depress prices for a few years, but eventually the hobby absorbs all of them and prices begin to exceed their old levels. Lately, discoverers of hoards of buttons have been clever enough to let them dribble out slowly over the years. Yet no one can keep such an exciting find a complete secret and rumors get out.

The best way to avoid overpaying for political items is to follow the items you like before buying them. After a few months of watching prices in a few political auctions you will know what prices are fair and what levels your favorite buttons usually reach.

Ted Hake's three volume *Encyclopedia of Political Buttons* is the most comprehensive listing of political items available and the 2004 price guide is relatively accurate. But prices change so quickly that no catalog could give you a completely accurate value. If a person has a handful of an item he may price it below the catalog value to sell them quickly. If a button has not been seen for sale for many years a seller may ask double or triple the catalog price.

If you are buying political items with an eye to investment, one thing to realize is that like with most collectibles buying the best is usually the most profitable. One hundred dollars spent on one rare item in excellent condition will usually go up faster than 10 items at $10 each.

For example, the price of a large colorful fob picturing James Cox was $125 in 1974, while a pewter stud with his name on a rooster was $10. Today the fob is worth about $5000 while the stud is $25.

If you can't afford the very best the next best choice is to collect what is likely to be popular. Colorful celluloid buttons are the most popular political item today and as more collectors begin collections there will be greater demand for them. Popular figures such as John F. Kennedy and Teddy Roosevelt attract many collectors.

While contemporary politicians are always considered flawed, their stature grows greatly after their passing. Depending on your politics, and how you expect the future to judge them, Johnson, Nixon, Ford, Carter, Reagan, Clinton or either of the Bushes might be good collections to start building today.

In any case, if you spend $50 or $100 on some political items, rather than on a dinner out or a round of golf, you'll have a lot more twenty years from now than a vague memory!

Some Sample Price Changes

George Washington Button
1970s $300-450
2000s $1500-2500

McKinley Roosevelt Button
1970s $10-12
2000s $100-125

Polk Dallas Poster 1840
1970s $75-100
2000s $400-600

Cox pewter stud 1920   Cox colorful button 1920
1970s $10-12   1970s $75-100
2000s $20-25   2000s $800-1000

Landon Knox Button
1970s $25-30
2000s $200-300

Lincoln Ambrotype 1860
1970s $700-1000
2000s $15,000-25,000

Stevenson Sparkman Button
1970s $10-15
2000s $60-80

Care and Storage

Most collectors keep their button collections in black cardboard boxes with glass tops. These are commonly known as "Riker mounts" or butterfly boxes. They are about 3/4 of an inch deep and filled with cotton or a similar substance. The most popular sizes are 12 x 16 inches and 8 x 12 inches. Buying them by the case will cut the cost consider-

MacArthur Collection
in 12 x 16 inch box

ably. The APIC has some vendors who offer them very cheaply to members.

Some collectors start with an 8 x 12 inch box for each election, then when they get full, to one 8 x 12 for each candidate, then moving up to the 12 x 16 inch size when the 8 x 12s get full.

RFK Collection
in 8 x 12 inch box
with velvet

To make them look even better, you can use colored fabric over the white cotton. Black velvet looks especially nice, especially with older items. For more valuable items you may want to buy more expensive wooden cases. Sometimes these are available with wooden cabinets in which to store them.

Campaign stamps, stickers, and other small paper items can be mounted on pages made for stamp or baseball card collectors. Be sure any items of this type that you buy are of archival quality and will not damage the items. Do not use wax-based photo albums (sometimes called "magnetic") or anything that was not made for collectibles or your collection may be destroyed.

There are special plastic holders that are good for post cards and other paper items. These can be purchased from hobby supply dealers. Most larger hobby shows have at least one dealer selling these items.

FDR Stamps
on stamp page

Protection

The two biggest risks to collectibles are moisture and insects. If you live in a humid area of the country and have a valuable collection you might want to use a dehumidifier near your collections once in a while. Many items have been destroyed when stored in an attic, garage or basement, so if that is your only choice be sure to pack them in waterproof containers. But keep in mind that extreme heat and cold can also damage them.

Sunlight can also damage all types of political items. If you display them in your home or office, be sure the sun does not shine directly on them. Even indirect sunlight can damage some items, so you should rotate your items on display and not leave any item exposed to light for too long. Many beautiful old items have been destroyed by too much light.

Your most valuable items should be kept in a safe deposit box at a bank. In order to still enjoy them you can make color photocopies of them which can be cut out and put in the trays at home with your cheaper buttons.

Duplicates

Duplicate buttons offered for sale are also kept in Riker mounts, or in 3-ring binders. The 3-ring binders can be used with vinyl coin pages and 2 x 2 inch coin holders or with cardboard pages. When using cardboard or paper with buttons, be sure to buy only acid-free paper or the acid in the paper will cause the buttons to rust. Acid-free paper and cardboard is available through archival supply houses.

For those with large quantities of duplicates, the above methods may require too much work or expense. Most collectors keep their quantity items in plastic bags or in drawers in plastic parts cabinets. **Warning:** Litho buttons are very easily scratched by each other. For this reason they should be mounted on paper or cardboard as soon as you acquire them. Some collectors mount litho buttons on sheets of plastic.

Cleaning

To remove dirt and restore the luster to celluloid buttons, many collectors use a product called Simichrome cream. It greatly enhances the appearance of the buttons and occasionally can restore a damaged-looking button to new. But do not use it on litho buttons or on celluloid buttons with cracks or pinholes or it will cause damage.

Most litho buttons can be cleaned with a moist cloth and mild soap. But be careful, older ones, especially if they have been in the sun, may lose their color from even light rubbing with a moist cloth.

Safes

Since most common burglars do not know the value of political items, you might not need a safe, but if you have a valuable collection you might want the extra protection a safe offers. Because of the risk of a broken water pipe or flooding, an in-floor safe is not a good idea. For a quantity of Riker mounts a large gun safe is ideal.

Beware of fire safes. The way fire safes work is to release water on the contents when the heat rises. This could permanently damage your collection. Better to place the safe in a corner against a concrete wall where risk of fire is lowest. But a basement or garage is dangerous because the humidity and temperature changes could damage the items.

Insurance

It may be difficult to get adequate coverage for your collection under a standard homeowner's or tenant's policy. It is important that you confirm with your insurance agent that your collection is covered for its full value. It may have to be specifically listed.

If you cannot insure it through your policy, and a separate policy through your agent is too expensive, there are other options. In recent years insurance agents have begun offering collectibles policies nationally. Some offer them to anyone, other to members of collectors' groups such as APIC or APS (American Philatelic Society). Some agents advertize in collectibles publications.

Fakes and Reproductions

Like most collectibles which have become valuable, rare political buttons have been counterfeited. But with a little experience most fakes are easy to detect. After a few years collecting, you can tell most fakes at a glance. But there are some deceptive ones and even long time collectors get fooled.

Luckily, most fakes are known and APIC has cataloged most of them. One APIC research project, *Brummagem: A Handbook on Fakes, Fantasies & Repins*, is available free from their web site (www.apic.us). More updated material will also be available through their web site, but only to members.

Before you pay a high price for a political item you should either check whether it may be a fake or be sure the dealer guarantees it. The political auctioneers all guarantee their items and APIC members are forbidden to sell fakes, so buying from these are safe. But buying on eBay or from an antique shop an be risky if you are not knowledgeable.

Occasionally an auctioneer or long time collector can be fooled by an item, so checking the Brummagem book and updated APIC materials can also be useful in the beginning.

This chapter will explain the most common fakes on the market and list items known to have been faked.

Button Sets

The most common fake buttons were manufactured as advertising giveaways by Kleenex and the American Oil Co. These are sets of buttons with one for each candidate from the Democratic and Republican parties. While the buttons of recent candidates look similar to real buttons, the older ones are obvious fakes because they are lithographed, whereas lithographs did not exist before about 1920. Another giveaway is that on the back edge they usually state "AO-1972" or "repro 1968," or "reproduction."

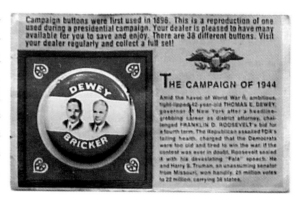

Fakes from these sets can be found in many antique stores and often unscrupulous owners have either scratched off or painted over the inscription on the edge. Some have even intentionally caused them to rust to try to trick buyers into thinking they are old.

Real   Fake   Real   Fake   Real   Fake

Fantasies

While a fake button is a copy of a real button, a fantasy is a button which never existed during the campaign. These are modern creations made to look like old buttons, but designed without copying a real button.

If you come across a button which is not in any catalog or auction there is a chance that you have found a rare undiscovered variety, but also a chance that you have come across a fantasy button. Check with the APIC brummagem project or a knowledgeable collector.

Repins

While searching for old campaign buttons, collectors have occasionally discovered caches of old button papers which were printed but never made into buttons. Some of those collectors thought the papers would be worth more if made into buttons. Buttons made long after an election, from original papers are called repins, and are in the same category as fakes and reproductions. Sometimes button manufacturers used old papers to make up buttons years after an election. In the 1930s a manufacturer in Baltimore was still making and selling buttons from the 1904 Roosevelt – Parker campaign.

One way to easily tell a repin is to look at the metal on the back. If the button design is from the 1930s, 40s or 50s and the metal is painted white on the back, it is a repin. This is known because white-backed metal was not used on any buttons until the 1960s. The source of this metal is venetian blind slats. Of course if the button is from a 1960s campaign, white metal on the back does not mean that it is a fake. Not all repins have white metal backs, but the backs of repins are usually different from the originals. Notice the rounded metal rim on the real Harding button below, compared to the angular metal rim on the repin.

Original
front and back

Repin
front and back

Another way to tell a repin is the surface of the button. Beginning in the 1890s buttons were made of celluloid, but in later years manufacturers switched to acetate and other plastics. After seeing and feeling buttons from different years you should be able to tell if a button is made of the right material.

Early tokens and medals

Original dies were used to make restrikes of many campaign tokens beginning in the middle of the 19th century. It is very hard to tell a restrike from an original unless it has been made on the wrong metal. The book, *American Political Badges and Medalets* lists most known varieties and known restrikes.

Known fakes to watch out for

The sets of fake buttons explained previously include all buttons from 1896 to the modern campaigns and are relatively easy to detect. The following are more difficult fakes.

Washington. Reproductions of the Washington Inaugural buttons have come from several sources over the last 130 years. In both 1876 and 1889 reproductions were made as commemorative items, and others have made them since then.

Jefferson through Bryan tokens and medals. Many, but not all restrikes are blank on the back. Many are made of lead, but copper, brass, iron and white metal have also been used. There is a restrike of a Lincoln Hamlin jugate medal which was made as a commemorative in 1961.

Fremont and Dayton. A celluloid button with an ornate ribbon was made as a commemorative 50 years after his campaign.

Pre-1896 buttons. The celluloid pinback political button did not exist until 1896. (They were patented in 1894.) And the lithograph button did not exist until about 1920. So all celluloid and lithographed buttons purporting to be from before 1896 are either fakes or commemoratives.

Teddy Roosevelt. There is a button picturing Roosevelt in his Rough Rider outfit with a flag behind him and the wording, "Teddy is Good enough for me" made both celluloid and lithographed.

Cox. A black on white "ELECT COX ROOSEVELT 1920" ribbon is known to be a fake because it was made on acetate cloth which did not exist in the 1920s.

Coolidge. A "Keep Coolidge" stamp with a fan is a fake if it does not have the copyright symbol (©). There is a white Coolidge beer bottle, and a black plastic ash tray which are not from the era. Any Coolidge buttons, bumper stickers or posters that say "The Red Garter" are from a bar in San Francisco.

Franklin Roosevelt. "Brewery Workers Choice" button in acetate rather than celluloid is a repin.

Fobs. There are matching solid brass 1-1/2 inch brass fobs picturing Bryan and Kern, and Taft and Sherman.

Bumper Stickers. Since adhesive-backed bumper stickers were not made until the 1950s, any bumper stickers from prior to that time are fantasy items.

Convention Tickets. There is a set of fake convention tickets. All have the stubs missing and no printing on the backs.

Convention Media Buttons. The 2 by 3 inch rectangular ABC news buttons for the 1976 Democratic and Republican conventions are said to be reissues if they have a pastel background (blue, green, yellow, orange) rather than the original white background.

Glassware. There are reproductions of both flasks and dishes. If you are not knowledgeable about these you should buy only from reputable dealers. An experienced collector can tell from the look of the glass and the sound when tapped.

Posters. There are at least two sets of full size posters and one set of mini posters covering several elections. When you see matching posters from different elections, that is a giveaway. But some have been artificially aged and when seen alone can be deceiving.

Fake Posters

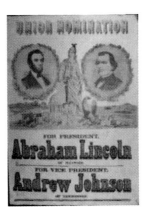

Match Holder. There is a fake of a match holder picturing Horace Greeley. (A match holder is a small metal container attached to the wall to hold wooden matches.) The fake is wired together rather than riveted. There may also be a matching fake of the Grant match holder from the same election.

Match Covers. The only known fake match covers are for Al Smith and Jimmy Walker issued by a night club to bring back the 1920s atmosphere.

Ribbons. A set of 19th century political ribbon reproductions was distributed in the 1960s. All are printed on acetate. Included are Harrison, Grant, Hayes/Wheeler, Tilden/Hendricks, Garfield, Cleveland, McKinley and Taft. Most have adhesive on the back from having been mounted on a display board.

Tabs. A set of 2 inch round tabs was distributed by Segrams. They picture Teddy Roosevelt, Wilson, Coolidge, Franklin Roosevelt, and Ike, and there are two slogan ones, "Keep Coolidge" and "I Like Ike."

How to Sell Your Political Items

If you have political items to sell, the way to get the best price for them is to auction them to the highest bidder. You have two ways to do this, through an auctioneer, or by yourself.

Political Auctioneer

If you have really great items worth at least a thousand dollars you may want to consign them to a political auctioneer who can put them in his catalog which will go to the most active collectors in the hobby. You will pay a commission of from ten to twenty percent, but you will probably get a higher price for your material than if you auction it yourself.

The most well known auctioneers are listed in Appendix 1. You should check with a few to compare their fees and how your material will be presented. If you have a large enough collection the auctioneer might issue a catalog just for your collection and put your photo in it. Some auctioneers have Internet bidding as well as phone and mail bidding and some picture the items on their web sites.

If you have a really great item such as a Cox-Roosevelt jugate the auctioneer might auction it without charging you a commission since the buyer would pay a good commission and the publicity of auctioning the items would be good for his auction.

Auctioning Yourself

The advent of eBay has made it possible for people with one or two items to present them to millions of potential customers and get the highest price. In order to get the best price on eBay you must make sure your item is seen by as many potential customers as possible. Here are some rules for getting better results on eBay:

•*Describe it correctly*. Some people search just for certain candidates or look only for certain words in the titles. Titling your listing "Political campaign button" will not get as many interested lookers as "John W. Davis 1924 picture button" because many collectors don't have time to look at every political lot.

•*Put it in the right category*. You should search for items like yours and see if anyone else is already selling one like it. This will tell you both the approximate value and where it gets the best bids.

•*Use a good photo*. You will get a lot more for an item if people can see what they are buying. With an unclear or poor photo, some people might assume the item is damaged and bid less.

•*Offer fair shipping terms*. Some sellers on eBay only ship Priority Mail because the boxes and envelopes are free. But small items would get there just as fast by first class mail for 60¢ which is $3.25 less than Priority Mail. Buyers will bid less for your item if they have to overpay on postage. (Tracking is 45¢ for Priority Mail and 55¢ for first class mail.)

Besides eBay you can auction your items yourself by advertising them in the *Political Bandwagon*, the monthly paper that goes to every member of American Political Items Collectors. This can be better or worse than eBay. You will reach serious collectors who do not have time for eBay, but many collectors don't read the *Bandwagon* carefully either. If you have especially rare items, advertising your upcoming eBay auction in the *Bandwagon* might get the best bidders from both worlds.

Advertising

If you have a quantity of items and you know how much they are worth, you can reach lot of collectors by advertising for sale at a fixed price in the *Political Bandwagon* or *Political Collector*.

Deciding What to Collect

Button from each
party, 1968

As with other types of collections, such as stamps and coins, most collectors start out collecting everything they can find, and later, when the impossibility of owning everything becomes apparent, narrowing down to a specialty.

What you specialize in will most likely be determined by your budget, how much room you have to store or display your collection, and your political inclinations. Some collectors fill their den or business office with their collection, others have them in every room of their homes. Some collectors even have special hurricane-proof rooms built on their homes to protect their collections from tornadoes and hurricanes.

If you don't have much room, then small buttons and stamps and stickers will give you the most variety in the least space. If you have plenty of space you can venture into banners, posters, clocks, torches and other 3-D items. If you really have a lot of space you can buy some life size manikins on which to display political clothing!

Token and Ballot from
each party, 1856

The following is a list of some of the most popular types of collections
- A button from every presidential ticket
- A jugate button from every presidential ticket
- A poster from every presidential ticket
- A jugate poster from every presidential ticket
- A display case from every presidential election
- A display case from every presidential candidate

Most collectors start with 20th century candidates because they are the easiest to find, and when those are nearly complete, begin on the 19th century.

Other than collecting a representation from each election, collectors usually specialize either by candidate or by type of item. For example, someone might specialize in either Ronald Reagan or Bill Clinton, depending on their political inclination, or they might specialize in political jewelry, or bumper stickers, or six inch buttons, or match book covers.

Depending on your personality you might prefer to collect what is most popular, or what is least popular. If you collect the most popular items you'll have to bid against a lot of other collectors, but they will probably continue to be in demand and rise in value. If you collect the least popular items, you'll usually get them at bargain prices with little competition. But when you decide to sell your collection there may still be little interest in them. However, many unpopular collectibles have become much more popular over time. If you were to assemble the premier collection in the field and publish a catalog of it, you may ignite its popularity.

Some of the most popular personalities to collect are:

Abraham Lincoln	Dwight D. Eisenhower
Teddy Roosevelt	John F. Kennedy
Eugene V. Debs	Ronald Reagan
Franklin D. Roosevelt	Bill Clinton

Some political personalities who are also popular are:

Benjamin Butler	Douglas MacArthur
Champ Clark	Eugene McCarthy
Admiral Dewey	Robert F. Kennedy
Alf Landon	Jimmie Carter
Wendell Willkie	George W. Bush

1948 Truman
collection

Some of the causes which are most popular are:

Woman Suffrage	Union Organizing
Prohibition	Early Communist and Socialist

Other categories that are popular are:

Third Party Items	Local Candidates
Hopefuls	

2003 Schwarzenegger
collection

Some personalities and causes which are not so popular at this time are:

Walter Mondale	Bob Dole
Michael Dukakis	Al Gore
George H. W. Bush	Desert Storm items
H. Ross Perot	

As you can see, many of these are losing presidential candidates. But items for the biggest losers of the first half of the 1900s, James Cox and John Davis are the rarest items of the century.

The following are types of items that are especially popular. To collect these you will need to compete with many others and often pay a premium.

19th century jugates	Jugate buttons
19th century flags	Colorful graphic buttons

The following is a list of some items which are underpriced relative to their scarcity. You can obtain these items relatively cheap compared to buttons or other items for the same candidate.

19th century ballots	Emery boards
19th century tokens	Jewelry
Brochures	Matchbooks
Bumper stickers	Pennants

The following section of the book shows some examples of items from specialized collections. These will let you know what is available and what kind of prices they command.

Specialized Collections

Hopefuls

A hopeful is a person who hoped to get his party's presidential nomination. Buttons for hopefuls are often less expensive than those of nominees and presidents, but some are very expensive. Because the names of many hopefuls have been forgotten, their buttons can sometimes be obtained very inexpensively. Appendix 2 in this book is a list of presidential hopefuls from 1789 to 2004.

A 50-80	B 10-20	C 80-120	D 15-25 / E 30-50
F 20-30	G 20-30	H 20-30	I 12-20 / J 15-25 / K 10-20
L 1-3 / M 4-6	N 2-4 / O 2-4	P 5-10 / Q 1-3	R 8-12
S 20-30	T 1-3	U 8-12	V 2-4

A   4-6

B   4-6

C   3-6

D   2-4

E   3-6

F   3-6

G   1-3

H   1-2

I   1-2

J   2-3

K   1-2

L   1-2

M   1-3

N   1-3

O   50¢-1

P   1-2

Q   2-4

R   2-4

S   2-4

T   2-4

U   3-6

V   2-4

W   4-8

X   2-4

A   2-4

B   2-5

C   1-3

D   10-20

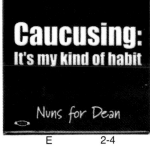

E   2-4

F   1-3

G   50¢-1

H   2-3

I   1-2

J   2-3

K   2-3

L   2-3

M   1-3

N   2-3

O   50¢-1

P   3-6

Q   2-3

R   5-10

S   2-3

Third Parties

Unbeknownst to many Americans, hundreds of thousands, sometimes millions of our fellow citizens vote for presidential candidates who are not members of the Democratic or Republican parties. These parties include Socialists, Nazis, Prohibitionists, Vegetarians, as well as more mainstream groups such as Libertarians and Greens. Many programs of the major parties started out as third party proposals. When a third party idea gets popular enough, one of the major parties adopts it on its platform and then the third party dies out. Third party items are very popular and it is a real challenge to find an item for each election for each party.

A   150-250   B   200-300   C   200-300   D   25-50   E   20-40   F   15-25

G   40-60   H   30-50   I   25-50   J   175-225   K   20-40   L   20-40   M   40-60

N   1-2   O   40-60   P   2-4   Q   4-7   R   2-4

S   4-8   T   3-6   U   1-3   V   3-6

A   50-100

B   12-18

C   10-20

D   10-20

E   10-15

F   100-150

G   30-60

H   10-20

I   5-10

J   20-30

K   10-20

L   20-30

M   25-35

N   5-10

O   5-10

P   5-10

Q   30-50

R   15-25

S   10-20

T   4-8

U   2-4

V   4-8

W   4-8

X   2-4

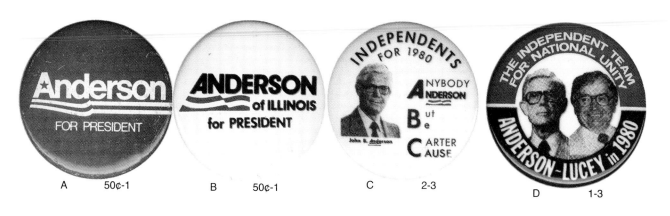

A   50¢-1   B   50¢-1   C   2-3   D   1-3

E   20-40
First Libertarian ticket
First woman to receive an electoral vote

F   3-6

G   8-12

H   1-2

I   4-8

J   3-6

K   1-3

L   2-4

M   2-4

N   1-3

O   1-3

P   2-4

Sets

Sets of similar buttons have been made at least since 1908. Most of them are state sets, but there are also nationality sets and foreign language sets.

A   20-30
           Each

B   10-20
           Each

C   10-20
           Each

D   10-15
           Each

E   1-3
           Each

F   1-3
           Each

G   2-4
           Each

H   1-2
           Each

I   1-2
           Each

J   4-8
           Each

K   1-3
           Each

L   50-100
           Set

M   50-100
           Set

N   1-3
           Each

O   30-50
           Set

P   50-100
           Set

Q   50-100
           Set

R   2-4
           Each

S   1-3
           Each

ALL 50 IN 1992!
FLORIDA
IS BUSH COUNTRY!
A   50-80
Set

VOTE '92
CALIFORNIA
IS FOR
CLINTON ★ GORE
B   50-80
Set

KANSAS
for
PEROT
STOCKDALE
1992
C   50-80
Set

NEW JERSEY
1996
DOLE ★ KEMP
D   40-60
Set

FLORIDA
IS FOR
CLINTON
GORE 96
E   40-60
Set

WASHINGTON
Supports
DOLE KEMP
President Vice-President
1996
F   40-60
Set

NORTH CAROLINA
For
DOLE
'96
G   40-60
Set

OHIO
Supports
CLINTON GORE
President Vice-President
1996
H   40-60
Set

RE-ELECT THE PRESIDENT
SOUTH DAKOTA
I   40-60
Set

INDIANA
For CLINTON
'96
J   40-60
Set

WISCONSIN
For
CLINTON
GORE
'96
K   30-50
Set

FLORIDA FOR
BUSH-CHENEY 2000
L   50-75
Set

FLORIDA FOR
GORE ·LIEBERMAN 2000
M   50-75
Set

FLORIDA GREENS
SUPPORT
Nader
LaDuke
2000
N   50-75
Set

FLORIDA LIBERTARIANS
for
Browne
Olivier
2000
O   50-75
Set

FLORIDA SOCIALISTS
SUPPORT
McReynolds
Hollis
2000
P   50-75
Set

Florida wants
Buchanan
Foster
Reform in 2000
Q   50-75
Set

Florida wants
Hagelin
Goldhaber
Reform in 2000
R   50-75
Set

KANSAS
IS FOR
BUSH
CHENEY
2000
S   50-75
Set

PENNSYLVANIA
IS FOR
Gore
Lieberman 2000
T   50-75
Set

WISCONSIN
Supports
BUSH
CHENEY
U   50-75
Set

OKLAHOMA
Supports
Gore 2000 Lieberman
V   50-75
Set

First Ladies

Since the 1940s there have been buttons issued for each of the First Ladies. There are a few for earlier ones, including Martha Washington, Dolly Madison and Francis Cleveland.

Few First Lady items have been produced, and they are usually not expensive, so the cost of collecting them is relatively reasonable. However, it is a challenge to find them. One interesting fact is that while there are many anti-Eleanor Roosevelt items, there are no known contemporary buttons supporting her.

A 10-20	B 20-30	C 15-20	D 20-40
E 2-4	F 2-4	G 2-4	H 2-4
I 2-4	J 2-4	K 2-4	L 2-4
M 4-8	N 2-4	O 2-4	

Candidates' Early Career Items

Many of our presidential candidates did not win on their first try. They lost a few times before winning the big one. And as a loser, their buttons were not considered very valuable so most were probably thrown away.

Consider Ronald Reagan. There are countless buttons available in large quantities from his 1980 and 1984 elections. But how often does a 1968 Reagan button come along? Or a 1972 Reagan? (Yes, there were at least 5 different types made, even though Nixon had a lock on the nomination.) And many were made for his 1976 attempt to wrest the nomination from President Ford. There is even a button and a stamp from Reagan's days as a Hollywood personality, and many gubernatorial items.

Nixon was elected to the House and Senate and lost both the presidency (1960) and the governorship of California (1962) before winning the presidency in 1968. John F. Kennedy was elected to the House and Senate, Truman ran for Judge and the Senate. Even Abraham Lincoln lost a few campaigns before winning the presidency. Their early buttons are sleeping gems waiting to be discovered and appreciated.

Impeachment Items

Since 1968 someone, somewhere, has suggested impeaching every president, and buttons have been produced for each of these causes.

The only two successful votes for impeachment in the House of Representatives were Andrew Johnson in 1868 and Bill Clinton in 1998 and tickets to those hearings are highly sought after.

A   8-12

B   3-6

C   2-4

D   1-2

E   2-4

F   3-6

G   1-3

H   1-3

I   2-4

J   2-4

K   2-4

L   1-3

M   1-3

N   2-4

O   200-1000+

P   2-5

Q   100-200+

Cause Items

There are cause items for every political position you can think of. The most sought-after are for prohibition and women's suffrage shown earlier in the book. But many people collect items from other causes such as these.

A   1-3

B   1-3

C   1-3

D   2-4

E   3-5
Pictured on LIFE magazine cover.

F   1-2

G   2-4

H   2-4

I   2-4

J   3-6

K   1-3

L   1-3

M   10-15

N   20-30

O   10-20

P   1-3

Q   50¢-2

A   8-15

B   15-25

C   2-4

D   2-4

E   3-6

F   1-3

G   4-8

H   2-4

I   1-3

J   2-4

K   2-4

L   6-12

M   2-4

N   10-20

O   20-30

P   10-20

Buttons with Stories

Many buttons have been made over the years which you can't understand without knowing about the event that inspired it. History buffs are big fans of these items. Interested collectors will often pay high prices for these items, but if you find them in a flea market or antique store they will usually be real cheap because few people know what they mean.

A   4000-5000

A controversial event in President Theodore Roosevelt's administration was his dinner with Booker T. Washington in the White House. This was at a time when the races were segregated, and some people were appalled that the president would invite a black man to dinner. Republicans issued buttons picturing this event to gain support in the black community, and some Democrats issued similar buttons to aggravate racists. The Democratic version of the button pictured Washington as bigger and blacker than the Republican button.

B   1000-1500

When officials of President Harding's administration were caught in fraudulent dealings over the Teapot Dome oil reserves, the scandal inspired some Democratic Party buttons in 1924.

C   20-25

One issue in the campaign of 1928 was the fact that Al Smith, the Democratic nominee, was a Catholic. No Catholic had ever been elected president and opponents of Smith used his religion as a scare tactic. Because some Protestants did not consider a Catholic to be a "Christian," the button above was issued.

D   5-10

When Franklin Roosevelt decided to run for a third term he was accused of wanting to start a dynasty and having royal ambitions.

E   15-20

At an event in Chicago during the 1940 presidential campaign some rotten eggs were thrown at Republican nominee Wendell Willkie.

F   6-12

This button is a take-off from a famous New Yorker cartoon in which a little girl looks at a plate of broccoli and says "I don't care it's still spinach to me."

G   6-12

This is a spelling of the way Franklin Roosevelt pronounced "war."

H   25-40

President Franklin Roosevelt once called Ambassador Joseph Kennedy (President Kennedy's father) "My Ambassador." This button is popular with both Roosevelt and Kennedy collectors.

I   10-20

Ma Perkins was Frances Perkins, Secretary of Labor, 1933-1945 and the first woman cabinet member. In 1939 a resolution was defeated in the House of Representatives to impeach her for not deporting Harry Bridges, a longshoreman leader and suspected communist.

J   6-12

In a discussion in 1944 over who should be the vice presidential nominee, Roosevelt had said, "Clear it with Sidney" Hillman, President of the CIO Political Action Committee which gave as much as 20 percent of the Democrats' $7 million campaign fund.

A   10-15

Roosevelt once went on a fishing trip by battleship.

B   10-15

This number represents the number of votes Thomas Dewey received in the 1944 Oregon primary election.

C   15-25

This button refers to the fact that President Truman built a balcony on the White House portico during his first term.

D   12-18

IGHAT has been said to stand for "I'm Gonna Hate All Trumans" but also "Ike's Gotta Have Another Term."

E   10-15

At the 1956 Republican national Convention every delegate voted for Richard Nixon for vice president except one disgruntled Nebraska delegate who voted a non-existent person names "Joe Smith." This inspired several buttons.

F   15-20

In a speech, President Kennedy once said that businessmen were "sons of bitches." Afterwards several groups of businessmen said they were proud to be SOBs and made up buttons to show it.

G   40-60

This is one of the most clever and obscure buttons made. It was issued to support Nixon's campaign for governor of California against Edmund. G. "Pat" Brown to insinuate he was a left-winger. The design means "Brown is pink."

H   3-6

When Robert F. Kennedy moved to New York to run for senator in 1964, some democrats opposed him because he wasn't really a New Yorker. This button supports Democrat Lyndon Johnson for president and Republican Charles Keating for senator.

I   5-10

This button is for the 26 million people who voted for Goldwater in 1964.

J   10-20

This slogan is a play on 1964 presidential candidate Barry Goldwater's slogan, "Extremism in pursuit of virtue is no vice."

K   15-25

This button jokes about the fact that President Lyndon Johnson was said to go around the White House turning off the lights to save electricity.

L   15-25

In 1965 Robert F. Kennedy was convinced to become the first person to scale Mt. Kennedy in Canada partly to combat his depression after his brother's assassination. The maker of this button apparently assumed that LBJ would run in 1968.

M   50-75

This button jokes about the fact that Nixon fired Archibald Cox, the special prosecutor who was investigating the Watergate scandal.

A   4-8

This button supported Edmund Sixtus Muskie, vice-presidential candidate with Hubert Humphrey in 1968, when he ran for president in 1972.

B   1-3

This button was for people who volunteered to work for George McGovern's 1972 campaign.

C   3-6

After Thomas Eagleton was chosen as McGovern's running mate in 1972 it was disclosed that he had undergone mental counseling and this became such a concern that he was forced to withdraw from the ticket. Many names were floated as replacements until Shriver was chosen.

D   300-600

E   6-12

Button "D" was issued in 1946 for Winston Churchill's appearance at Westminster College in which he gave his famous "Iron Curtain" speech. When Mikhail Gorbachev and George Bush appeared at the same college in 1992 some clever button makers came to the event and sold a similar button.

F   2-4

This button was made by Republicans who opposed John Anderson's 3rd party run against Ronald Reagan in 1980.

G   2-4

Because the word for "penis" in the Farsi language is pronounced "dole" and Iranian newspapers can't print this word, there was some concern as to what they would do if Dole was elected our president.

H   3-5

The background picture on this button is a bagel, since Lieberman was the first major party nominee to be Jewish.

I   1-3

In the 2000 election many people in Palm Beach County, Florida said they had accidentally voted for Pat Buchanan instead of Al Gore because the ballot was confusing. This button was for people who weren't confused by the ballot.

J   1-3

This figure is the number of popular votes by which Al Gore out-polled George W. Bush in the 2000 election. Bush won because he had more electoral college votes.

K   1-3

In the 2000 post-election chaos in which the winner was not determined for five weeks, William Daley was in charge of Al Gore's challenge to the Florida results. This button refers to the fact that Daley's father, Chicago Mayor Richard J. Daley, was alleged to have tampered with the results of the 1960 election that made Kennedy president.

L   3-5

One unique thing about Wesley Clark when he sought the Democratic nomination in 2004 was that he was a four star general. This button was made for his supporters.

Local Items

With each of the major presidential nominees inspiring hundreds of buttons, and older buttons rising to unprecedented price levels, more collectors than ever are taking up the collecting of items for candidates for state offices. Some collect only their own state. Others specialize in a certain time period, or interest such as women or African-American candidates.

The most popular are senator and governor buttons. Items for other offices such as congress and mayor are usually collected only by people in those states or cities.

While there may be several candidates for governor and senator, each usually has only one or a few buttons, and the lower demand keeps the prices of these reasonable.

A   10-20
B   1-2
C   3-6
D   2-4
E   10-20
F   1-2
G   2-4

H   2-4
I   2-4
J   1-3
K   4-8
L   3-6

M   4-8
N   2-4
O   2-4

P   2-4
Q   2-4
R   3-6
S   3-6

International Items

There are so many American political items to collect, and so few foreign items to be found in this country, that very few collectors take up collecting foreign items.

One exception is Soviet pins. During the Soviet regime, Russia and some of the other countries in eastern Europe issued hundreds, or possibly thousands of pins celebrating the Soviet system. Most likely these were used to keep the youth interested in communism and amused enough to forget their dire straights.

In recent years some of these items pictured or named U. S. presidents and collectors who specialize in those presidents are eager to obtain Soviet pins with their hero.

The author does not know of any catalog of foreign political items, so adding these to your collection would be a real challenge.

"Anti" Items

Items opposing a candidate are some of the most clever and entertaining. Many collectors who collect one candidate collect items which are against their opponents, but some even collect items against their hero. For more anti buttons see pages 118-120.

STOP THE BAKER INVESTIGATION! DON'T LET THE FACTS COME OUT! A 6-12	**DUMP HUMPH** B 2-4	HHHH 68 C 2-4	**STERILIZE LBJ:** NO MORE UGLY CHILDREN! D 10-15

NIXON'S THE ONE!!
E   25-50

Excerpt from **Dublin Dispatch** THE VOICE OF THE IRISH FREE WORLD GOD SAVES SENATOR KENNEDY AS GIRL DROWNS DEVOUT PAIR BELIEVED TO BE ON WAY TO MIDNIGHT MASS TED PRAYS FOR ALMOST NINE HOURS BEFORE LEAVING SCENE OF ACCIDENT IRISH GOVERNMENT BLAMES ITALIAN CONTRACTOR FOR FAULTY BRIDGE
F   5-10

KENNEDY FOR LIFE GUARD
G   2-4

REMEMBER **THE ALAMO!** REMEMBER **PEARL HARBOR!** BUT DON'T FORGET CHAPPAQUIDICK Read Back Side
H   4-8

The Carter Cocktail **AMERICA ON THE ROCKS**
I   2-4

JANE WYMAN WAS RIGHT
J   2-3

GARY HART WIN ONE FOR THE ZIPPER! 1988
K   2-4

AMERICANS FOR PEROT **UNITED** WE'RE **NUTS!**
L   2-4

REAGAN HOOD "ROB FROM THE POOR GIVE TO THE RICH"
M   10-20

PRES. REAGAN! Don't Trickle down on ME!
N   5-10

OOPS!
O   2-4

A   3-6

B   3-6

C   3-6
AMERICA DON'T STEP IN
Dukaka

D   5-10
VOTE FOR WALLY AND THE BEAVER IN '84

E   1-3
Read my lips...now!
TAXES

F   3-6
No Bush in '92!

G   1-3
JUST SAY NOE

H   3-6
I've Fallen And I Can't Get Up
BUSH APPROVAL RATING
Slogan is from a home emergency
device commercial.

I   2-4
Clinton
again?

J   4-8
End the Coverup!
Clinton with
Lee Harvey Oswald

K   2-3
Kerry Eats Quiche
With French Wine

L   2-4

M   5-10
CRUSH BUSH

N   2-4
REGIME CHANGE BEGINS AT HOME

Tabs

While some collectors ignore tabs, others specialize in them. The common tabs are among the cheapest items available for a candidate, but the rarer tabs reach relatively high prices. There has even been a book published devoted to political tabs but it is out of print. Because there are relatively few tabs, most tab collectors also include tab-like items such as tobacco tags and other fold-over metal items in their collections. Tabs are usually made of metal but early examples exist in paper, foil and celluloid.

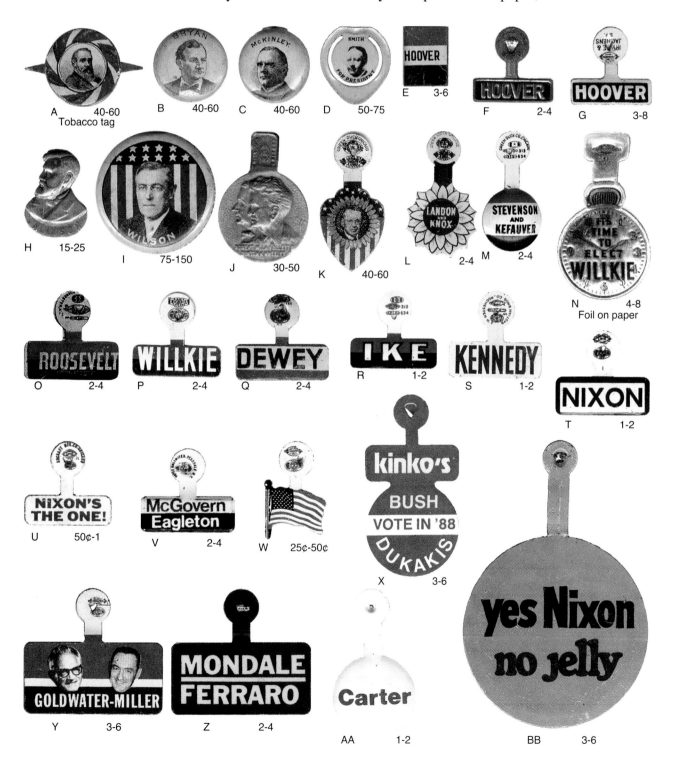

A 40-60 Tobacco tag
B 40-60
C 40-60
D 50-75
E 3-6
F 2-4
G 3-8

H 15-25
I 75-150
J 30-50
K 40-60
L 2-4
M 2-4
N 4-8 Foil on paper

O 2-4
P 2-4
Q 2-4
R 1-2
S 1-2
T 1-2

U 50¢-1
V 2-4
W 25¢-50¢
X 3-6

Y 3-6
Z 2-4
AA 1-2
BB 3-6

Flashers

For many years flashers were not so popular with collectors, but today they are more in demand and the rarer ones can command hundreds of dollars. There is even a flasher collectors' group in APIC.

A   25-50

B   10-20

C   10-20

D   15-25

E   10-15

F   3-6

G   4-8

H   2-5

I   3-6

J   3-6

K   3-6

L   4-8

M   5-10

N   3-6

O   6-12

6 and 9 Inch Buttons

Some collectors feel that six and nine inch buttons are too big to deal with but others specilize in them. Most collectors use them for centerpieces for their displays since they stand out from a distance.

6 inchers

A 50-75

B 15-20

C 8-12

D 10-15

E 12-20

F 5-10

G 12-20

H 10-15

I 10-15

J 6-12

K 10-15

L 20-40

M 10-60

N 5-8

O 6-12

9 inchers

P 600-1000

Q 75-100

R 50-75

S 125-250

T 20-40

U 15-20

V 20-30

W 10-20

Jewelry

Jewelry items are not as popular as pinback buttons, so they are much more reasonably priced than buttons of the same campaign. Specialists in particular campaigns usually include them with their button collection.

A   10-15

B   10-15

C   4-8

D   15-25
J. F. Kennedy's boat,
PT-109

E   5-10

F   2-4

G   5-10

H   3-6

I   2-4

J   2-4
Necklace

K   3-5

L   2-4

M   2-4

N   2-4

O   3-5

P   2-4

Q   3-6

R   8-12

S   20-30

T   20-30

U   2-4

V   2-4

W   1-2

X   6-12

Paper Items

Posters

While some collectors feel that political campaign posters are too large to enjoy, others use them to decorate their homes or offices. Because their size is a handicap to many, posters well over a hundred years old are still available at very reasonable prices.

The most reasonably priced posters were originally distributed as supplements to magazines and newspapers of the day. Because these were preserved in large quantities by both libraries and individuals, excellent copies can be found easily. Actual campaign posters, especially jugates, are more difficult to find and much more expensive.

A   75-150

B   100-200

C   50-100
From magazine

D   50-100

E   50-100

F   75-125

G   10-20

H   100-200

I   10-20

J   5-10

Jugate and picture posters

Here is a list of average prices of jugate and picture posters since 1844. A pair of matching president and vice-president candidate posters is often accepted as a jugate. Newspaper, magazine and book posters can be much cheaper than the prices here.

	Jugate	Picture			Jugate	Picture
1844 Polk	400-600	200-300		1928 Hoover	50-100	25-50
1844 Clay	400-600	200-300		1928 Smith	100-150	25-50
1848 Taylor	500-700	200-300		1932 Roosevelt	40-80	10-30
1848 Cass	600-800	200-400		1932 Hoover	50-100	15-30
1852 Pierce	600-900	200-300		1936 Roosevelt	50-100	10-30
1852 Scott	600-900	200-300		1936 Landon	75-150	15-30
1856 Buchanan	500-800	200-300		1940 Roosevelt	30-70	10-30
1856 Fremont	500-800	200-300		1940 Willkie	75-150	20-40
1856 Fillmore	500-800	200-300		1944 Roosevelt	75-150	10-30
1860 Lincoln	2500-5000	300-500		1944 Dewey	40-80	10-25
1860 Douglas	2000-4000	200-300		1948 Truman	75-150	50-100
1864 Lincoln	3000-7000	300-500		1948 Dewey	30-60	10-25
1864 McClellan	1000-2000	300-400		1952 Eisenhower	30-60	10-20
1868 Grant	500-1000	200-300		1952 Stevenson	40-80	15-30
1868 Seymour	1000-1500	200-300		1956 Eisenhower	30-60	10-20
1872 Grant	1500-2500	200-300		1956 Stevenson	30-60	15-30
1872 Greeley	1500-2500	300-500		1960 Kennedy	75-200	25-50
1876 Hayes	1500-3000	300-500		1960 Nixon	25-50	10-20
1876 Tilden	1500-3000	300-500		1964 Johnson	15-30	5-10
1880 Garfield	200-300	50-150		1964 Goldwater	15-30	5-15
1880 Hancock	200-400	50-150		1968 Nixon	10-20	5-10
1884 Cleveland	150-300	50-150		1968 Humphrey	8-15	5-10
1884 Blaine	150-500	50-150		1968 Wallace	15-25	5-10
1888 Harrison	75-150	50-100		1972 Nixon	8-15	5-10
1888 Cleveland	75-150	50-100		1972 McGovern	8-15	5-10
1892 Cleveland	75-150	50-100		1976 Carter	5-10	5-10
1892 Harrison	75-150	50-100		1976 Ford	10-20	5-10
1896 McKinley	75-150	50-100		1980 Reagan	10-20	8-15
1896 Bryan	75-150	50-100		1980 Carter	8-15	5-10
1900 McKinley	75-150	50-100		1980 Anderson	10-20	8-15
1900 Bryan	75-150	50-100		1984 Reagan	8-15	8-15
1904 Roosevelt	75-150	50-100		1984 Mondale	5-10	5-10
1904 Parker	100-200	75-150		1988 Bush	5-10	5-10
1908 Taft	75-150	30-60		1988 Dukakis	5-10	5-10
1908 Bryan	75-150	50-100		1992 Clinton	5-10	5-10
1912 Wilson	100-150	25-50		1992 Bush	5-10	5-10
1912 Taft	50-100	20-40		1992 Perot	10-20	5-10
1912 Roosevelt	100-200	30-60		1996 Clinton	5-10	5-10
1916 Wilson	100-150	25-50		1996 Dole	5-10	5-10
1916 Hughes	100-200	20-50		2000 Bush	8-15	5-10
1920 Harding	75-150	20-50		2000 Gore	8-15	5-10
1920 Cox	300-600	100-200				
1924 Coolidge	50-100	25-50				
1924 Davis	400-800	100-200				

Stamps

Political campaign stamps seem to get little respect. Stamp collectors don't consider them stamps, and political collectors do not consider them as desirable as buttons. Some rare examples have sold for over $500, but most are underpriced compared to buttons, considering to their scarcity and graphic appeal. The author of this book also wrote *Political Campaign Stamps* published by Krause Publications in 1998.

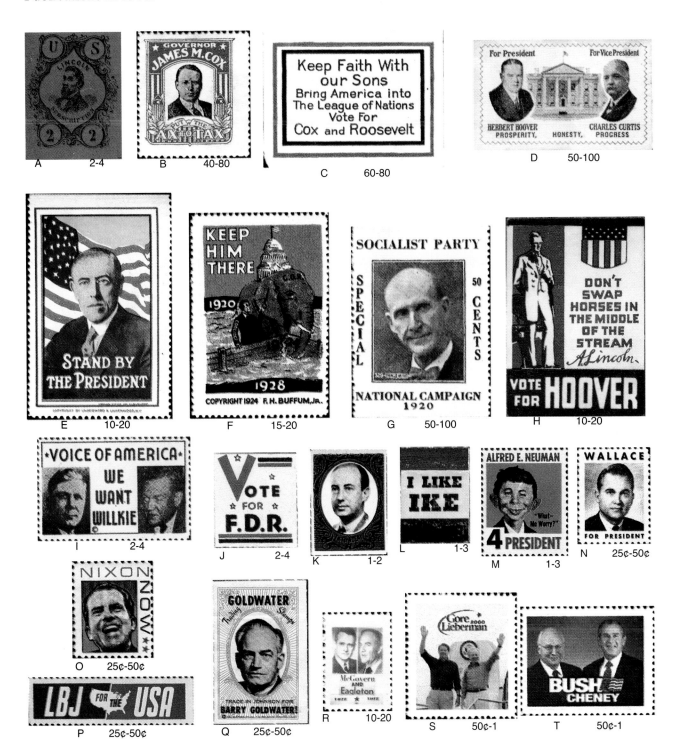

Ballots

If you would like to put together a collection of presidential campaign items going back to the 1820s the most affordable would be ballots. In the 19th century ballots which could be dropped in the ballot box on election day were printed in the newspapers for weeks or even months ahead of time. These are actual campaign items and since old newspapers are plentiful, they are very affordable. Most of the 19th century candidates' ballots can be found for $20 to $50. If you prefer to collect ballots which were printed individually, they cost a bit more but are still reasonable considering their age and scarcity.

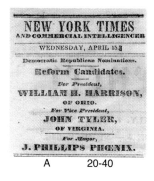

A   20-40

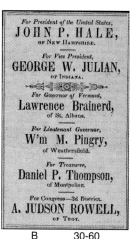

B   30-60

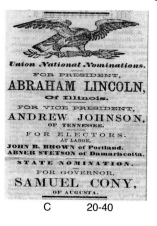

C   20-40

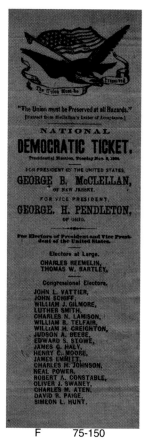

F   75-150

D   15-30

E   20-40

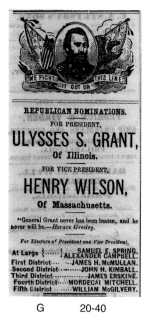

G   20-40

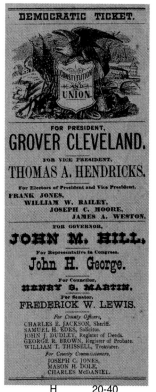

H   20-40

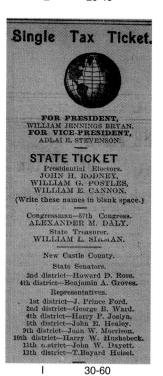

I   30-60

J   20-40

Inaugural Covers

Since at least 1929, collectors have made up special envelopes to be cancelled on inauguration day. The post office began using a special cancellation, and in recent elections has made them in attractive designs and available in several locations including the president's and vice-president's birthplaces. Collectors and vendors have designed artwork for these covers, called cachets, and many collectors attempt to obtain all cachets for a particular candidate.

By including ordinary envelopes from letters mailed by chance on inauguration day, one can compile a collection from every inauguration, but it would probably take a lifetime. Just make a list of the dates and check the "old letters" boxes at antiques stores and stamp dealers.

A	10-20	B	3-5	C	4-8
D	10-20	E	1-3	F	3-5
G	2-4	H	2-4	I	2-4
J	2-4	K	2-4	L	2-4
M	2-4	N	2-4	O	3-6

Stickers

Campaign stickers (self-adhesive, peel-and-stick, rather than gummed, lick-and-stick stamps) have been even less popular than campaign stamps. One problem is that the glue sometimes migrates through the paper causing unsightly stains. Fortunately, solvents can be used to dissolve the glue and restore the stickers to their original look without affecting the ink. With most campaigns today using stickers instead of buttons, these may become much more popular in the future.

Window stickers

Few people specialize in collecting window stickers, but those who collect particular candidates eagerly seek them, and stickers with good graphics or slogans are in demand by many collectors. They make great centerpieces for a display of buttons.

A   1000-1500

B   100-150

C   2-5

D   100-150

E   5-8

F   3-5

G   6-12

H   4-8

I   3-6

J   3-5

K   12-18

L   3-6

M   3-5

N   10-15

O   1-2

Bumper stickers

Bumper stickers also have few specialists, and again the most eager collectors seek out those for a special candidate.

A   1-3

B   1-3

C   2-4

D   1-3

E   1-2

F   1-3

G   50¢-1

H   50¢-1

I   50¢-1

J   1-3

K   50¢-1

L   1-2

M   1-2

N   3-5

O   3-6
From his congressional races

P   2-4

Q   1-3

R   50¢-2

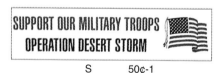

S   50¢-1

T   50¢-1

U   1-3

V   1-2

W   50¢-1

X   50¢-1

Y   50¢-1

Trading cards

Political trading cards probably have more adherents among non-sports card collectors in the trading card world than in the political hobby. Consequently, you can probably get more bargains at a political collectors' convention, and expect to pay more at a trading card convention.

A   4-8

B   5-10

C   6-12

D   5-10

E   10-20

F   1-3
From a game
Set   50-100

G   3-6

H   3-6

I   20-30

J   1-3

K   Deck 20-30
Deck of playing
cards

L   2-4

M   1-2

N   2-4

O   1-3

P   1-3

Q   1-3

R   1-2

S   2-4

T   2-4

Convention Tickets

There are many specialists in political convention tickets (and a catalog for them has been published both in paper and online versions), so they are not as cheap as most other paper items. But for their age and beauty they are bargains.

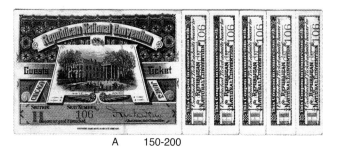

A   150-200

B   40-60

C   6-12

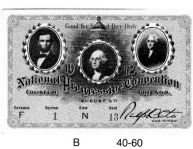

D   6-12

E   5-10

F   10-20

G   5-10

H   10-20

I   4-8

J   5-10

K   4-8

L   5-10

Mock Currency

There are many collectors of political campaign currency, that is, political leaflets designed like currency, but they are still relatively inexpensive and easy to find. Besides political shows, they can be found at coin and currency shows as well as paper and ephemera shows.

A   500-1000

B   20-30

C   5-10

D   20-40

E   4-8

F   40-60

G   1-3

H   4-8

I   2-4

J   1-3

K   1-2

L   1-3

M   1-3

N   1-3

O   1-3

P   1-2

Q   50¢-1

R   50¢-1

Post Cards

There is such a large group of post card collectors that political post cards are much more expensive than most political paper items. Rare cards can fetch thousands of dollars. Most postcard dealers have their stock well organized and researched, so bargains are rare at post card shows.

A 6-12	B 10-15	C 20-40	D 20-40
E 20-30	F 15-30	G 20-40	H 300-600
I 25-50	J 20-40	K 30-60	L 4-8 M 3-5 N 1-2
O 1-2	P 2-4	Q 1-2	R 1-2 S 1-2 T 1-3
U 1-2	V 1-2	W 2-4	X 1-3

Catalogs

Seeing $700 campaign pins priced at $7.50 per gross and $300 lanterns priced at 80¢ a dozen in a 1900 catalog is enough to make a grown collector cry. Why didn't our grandparents stash away a few dozen? Or one even? But catalogs of old campaign items are interesting collectibles. The fact that many items pictured in the catalogs are not found in any collection makes one wonder how many more items are waiting to be discovered.

A   75-150

B   100-175

C   30-50

D   30-50

E   15-25

F   15-25

G   6-12

H   10-15

I   10-15

J   10-20
1968 Trimble catalog

K   5-10

L   5-10

M   3-5

N   2-4

O   2-4

P   2-4

Cloth Items

Textiles are among the most attractive items in museum exhibits, yet because they require a lot of space to exhibit and store, they are not in a great demand among most collectors. For this reason they are still available at very reasonable prices.

Flags and Pennants

The best campaign flags are from the last century, however, there are many pennants available for candidates from the twentieth century. While the flags from the nineteenth century are among the most expensive political items, pennants are usually very inexpensive.

A 5000-10,000

B 15,000-20,000

C 4000-8000

DE 800-1200

E 800-1200

F 200-400

G 75-150

H 400-800

I 15-30

J 15-25

K 5-8

Bandannas, Scarves and Handkerchiefs

While many of them are more graphic than flags of the same age, bandannas are very reasonably priced in relation to their age and beauty.

A   200-400

B   150-300

C   300-500

D   75-100

E   35-75

F   15-30

G   35-65

H   20-40

I   15-30

J   20-40

K   15-30

L   10-20

Banners

While some antique dealers think bigger items are more valuable, because of the difficulty in displaying large items such as banners, their prices usually are lower than one might expect. While small beautiful banners command high prices, huge non-graphic banners are very reasonably priced. If you have a large house with a lot of empty wall space you can decorate those walls very reasonably!

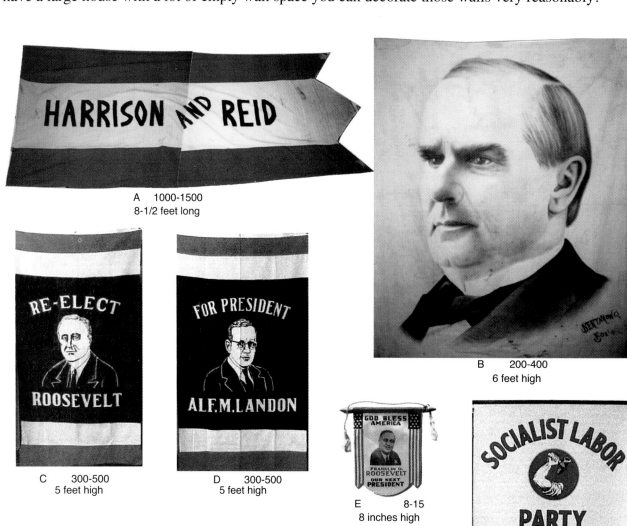

A   1000-1500
8-1/2 feet long

B   200-400
6 feet high

C   300-500
5 feet high

D   300-500
5 feet high

E   8-15
8 inches high

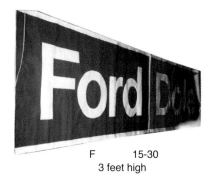

F   15-30
3 feet high

G   50-100
3 feet high

H   300-600
4 feet high

Ribbons

The most colorful and desirable ribbons are from the 19th century. Often they were made in multi-colored designs with pictures of the candidates. Recent ribbons are usually one color with gold printing and sell for only a few dollars.

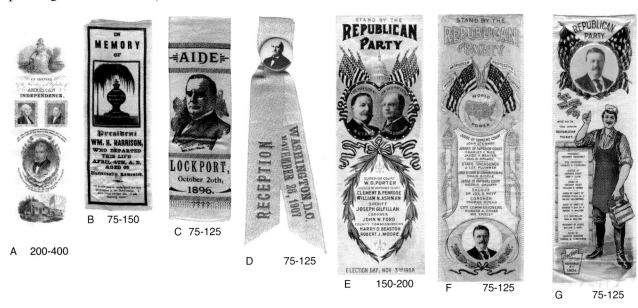

A   200-400

B   75-150

C 75-125

D   75-125

E   150-200

F   75-125

G   75-125

H   40-65

I   2000-3000

J   8-15

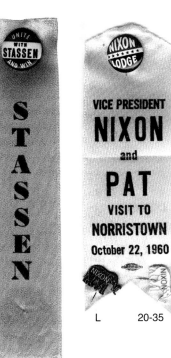

K   10-20

L   20-35

M   1-3

3-D Items

For some, three-dimensional items are the most exciting political collectibles. Old campaign torches and lanterns, and new toys and banks are pieces of Americana which are seldom seen outside of museums. They are especially nice if you display your collection in a local library or school. But because they are bulky and difficult to transport and store, they attract fewer collectors and seem underpriced compared to items of similar age.

The following are examples of some types of items that are available. For some items an entire book could be published showing hundreds of varieties, so what is shown here is extremely limited. The purpose is to show you what types of items are out there, the approximate scarcity and value, and perhaps kindle your interest in them.

There are very few books on items of this type. The best you can do is find small sections in larger books on similar collectibles such as clocks or paperweights. If you have an interest in anything pictured here, and an inclination to research and write, a book on the subject would fill a historical need.

Clocks and Watches

There are clocks and watches for presidents and presidential candidates going back to the beginning of our country. They are not easy to find, but the cost is a lot lower than for buttons of equal rarity.

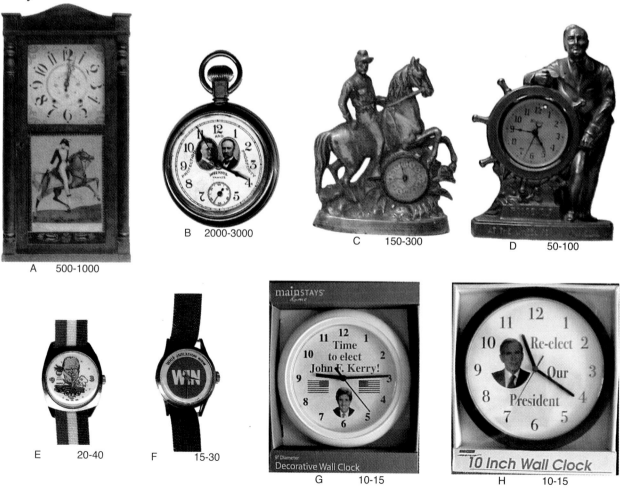

A   500-1000

B   2000-3000

C   150-300

D   50-100

E   20-40

F   15-30

G   10-15

H   10-15

Toys

Toys related to presidents and elections also go back to the beginning of our nation. There are also many varieties and the cost is low relative to their scarcity.

A   15-25

B   15-20

C   6-12

D   15-20

E   15-30

License Plate Attachments

There are hundreds of license plate attachments but few of them are inexpensive. There are many eager collectors and auction prices are rarely cheap. Most of them were made in the 1920s through 40s, and after that there are very few since they were replaced by bumper stickers. Condition is an important factor in value and rust, chips, dents and scratches can reduce value dramatically.

F   800-1200

G   25-40

H   50-75

I   20-40

J   20-40

Soap

There weren't many types of soap issued for presidential campaigns, and those that were probably served their function or disintegrated over the years. Thus, though not in the highest demand as political collectibles, they are not cheap when they appear.

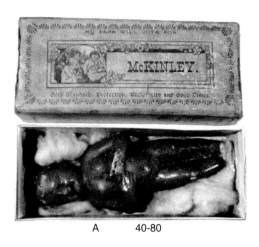

A   40-80

B   20-40

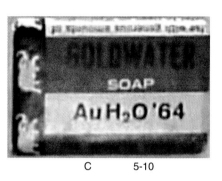

C   5-10

Plaques

Most plaques related to political figures are not campaign items, but commemorations of some type, and since most political collectors like campaign items, they are not in the highest demand. So, if you have the wall space, you can accumulate a nice selection of plaques from the last two centuries for a very reasonable sum.

D   300-500
Winfield Scott

E   30-60
James Garfield

F   100-150
Teddy Roosevelt
1904 World's Fair

G   50-100
Anti-Carrie Nation Hatchet

H   20-30

I   5-10

Noise Makers

There are not a lot of political noisemakers, and not many specialists in them, but collectors of particular candidates pay good prices for them.

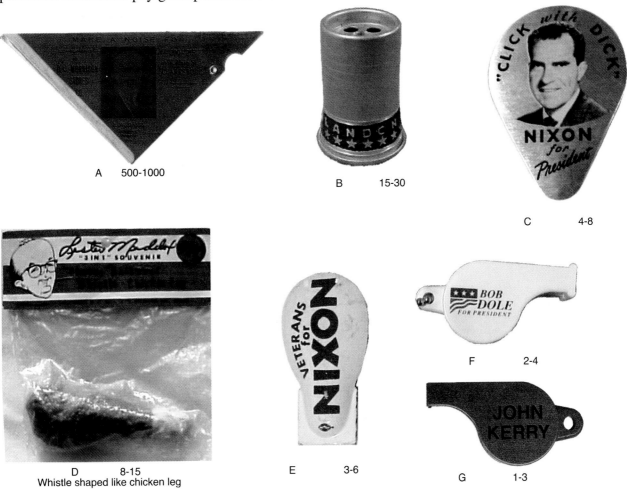

A   500-1000

B   15-30

C   4-8

D   8-15
Whistle shaped like chicken leg

E   3-6

F   2-4

G   1-3

Pens and Pencils

Political pens and pencils are usually relatively inexpensive, except for those for candidates whose items are especially rare.

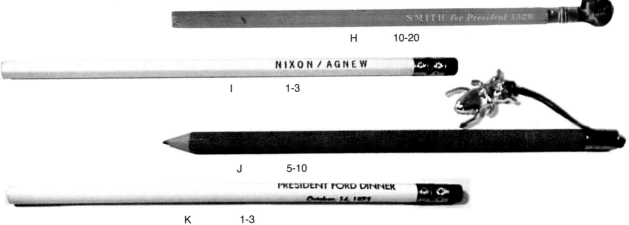

H   10-20

I   1-3

J   5-10

K   1-3

Cans, Cups, Mugs

Since they are not the easiest to store, larger 3-D items such as these are relatively inexpensive. But they are great display items if you have the space.

A   50-100

B   10-20

C   5-10

D   20-40
Said to have been seized by secret service agents in an abuse of discretion

E   3-5

Fans

Before air conditioning, fans were necessary items at crowded political meetings.

F   75-125

G   30-60

H   15-30

I   3-6

Pocket Knives

Both knife collectors and political collectors seek political pocket knives, but there are not a lot of varieties, so few are found in political collections. Reproductions are common.

J   100-200

K   15-30

L   5-10

Kitchen Items

Useful household items have almost always been given out as political favors.

A   5-8
Trivet

B   2-4
Coffee scoop

C   2-4
Pot holder

Paper Weights

Paper weights were used both as campaign items and as souvenirs. The former are often quite rare and expensive and the latter less desirable.

D   75-125

E   75-125

F   1500-3000

G   20-40

Sound Recordings

Sound recordings began about 100 years ago, but there are very few which are actual campaign items. Speeches by presidents are more common.

H   75-125
Teddy Roosevelt

I   50-100
James Cox

J   5-10
Barry Goldwater

K   4-8

Trays

There have not been many political trays made. Most of them are from the 1896-1912 era. But they make nice display pieces.

D   50-100

A   75-150

B   400-700

C   200-300

E   40-60

Unusual Items

Among the political collectibles one can find many unusual items, many of which were only made for one or a few elections. The following are campaign items which were made for at least one but not more than a few presidential campaigns.

Lady's Compact

E   50-100

Mouse Pads

F   5-10

G   5-10

Comb

H   100-150

Telephone cord

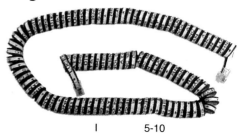

I   5-10

Seat Cushion

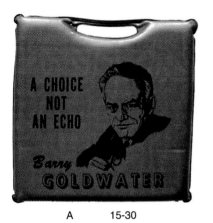

A   15-30

Bed Pan

B   10-20

Chimney Flue Cover

C   40-80

Bank

D   15-30

Yo-yo

E   3-6

Fly Swatters

F   5-10 pair

Sewing Needles

G   20-40

Tattoos

H   2-4

Frisbee

I   4-8

Paper Cube

A   5-10

Antenna Ball

B   2-4

Coin Pouch

C   2-4

Fishing Lure

D   5-10

Light Switch Cover

E   3-6

Candy Container

F   300-600

Glossary

Like any hobby, political item collecting has certain terms which make it easier to discuss common objects which are hard to describe.

APIC. (pronounced eh-pee-eye-see; only pronounved ay-pick by newbies) American Political Items Collectors, the collector organization formed in 1945 to promote collecting political campaign items.

Back paper. A piece of paper inserted into the back of a celluloid button, usually with the name of the manufacturer.

Bourse. The sales room at a political collectors convention where dealers set up tables to sell their items.

Broadside. An advertisement usually printed on paper (though sometimes on cloth), usually on one side (but sometimes on both sides and folded).

Brummagem. A fake political item.

Celluloid. A button made by putting a piece of clear celluloid over a printed button paper, wrapping it around a metal shell and crimping it in the back around a metal collet. Today other materials such as vinyl, mylar and plastic are used but the buttons are still called celluloids, or cellos.

Coattail. A political item supporting one or more local level candidates along with the presidential candidate.

Curl. The back edge around a button.

Daguerreotype. A photograph produced on a thin sheet of brass, popular in the 1840s.

Disclaimer. A statement printed on a political item stating who distributed it.

Fantasy. An item which was made years after an election, which is not a reproduction, using a design which was never used during the election.

Ferrotype (also **ferro**). A photograph produced on a thin sheet of iron invented in the 1850s. Also used to describe political tokens and badges which contain a ferrotype photograph.

Flasher. An item, usually a button in which the picture alternates when viewed from different angles.

Foxing. Spots that develop on celluloid buttons when the metal under the paper starts to rust, discoloring the paper. Can also describe spots on paper items.

Jugate. (pronounced joo-get) An item which pictures two persons, usually the presidential and vice-presidential nominees. Items picturing senator and governor candidates or a presidential candidate and a lower office candidate would also be jugates.

Litho. A button made by lithographically printing the button design directly on a sheet of metal (often called tin, but actually iron). The button is then punched out and then curled on the edges to hold the pin.

Mechanical. An item such as a button or post card which has a moving part which usually changes the words or picture.

Medal. A solid metal political item similar to a coin, sometimes holed to be worn suspended by a pin.

MFA. "Mentioned for accuracy" Used in political auctions when describing a flaw in an item which might be overlooked by some purchasers but which could be a reason for other purchasers to return the item if not mentioned.

Multigate. An item picturing five or more candidates.

Quadrugate. An item picturing four candidates.

Repin. A button manufactured using some or all original materials, but made after the time of an election.

Room hopping. Visiting hotel rooms of political dealers offering items for sale when attending a political collectibles show.

Sniping. Bidding on an item in an auction in the last seconds.

Stud. A button with a small metal disk attached to the back for putting through a button hole. Most common from 1884-1900.

Tab. A flat piece of lithographed metal which has (naturally enough) a tab at the top which can be folded over to attach the item to a collar, lapel or pocket. Many tab collectors include similar items such as tobacco tags in their collections. Some tabs are made of paper, metal foil on paper, or celluloid.

Trigate. An item picturing three candidates.

Union bug. The official symbol of a labor union, placed on a campaign item during manufacture to indicate it was made by union labor.

Appendix 1: Resources

This appendix includes sources of further information for collectors of political items.

Organizations

There is only one organization for collectors of political campaign memorabilia, the American Political Items Collectors. This is a nonprofit educational organization that was formed in 1945 and has 2000-3000 members. (Membership fluctuates with the highest number during presidential election years and dropping each of the next three years until it again peaks in the next election year.)

Dues, which were recently $30, are now as low as $8 a year (going up to $28) depending on how many membership benefits you desire. The higher dues includes a monthly newspaper the *Political Bandwagon,* and a quarterly magazine.

The APIC web site is at: http://www.apic.us

Specialty Chapters

Within APIC there are special chapters for people interested in the following types of items. By joining APIC you can also join the chapter(s) of your choice.

George W. Bush	Al Gore	Republican Items
Jimmy Carter	Kennedy	Franklin D. Roosevelt
Cause Items	John Kerry	Theodore Roosevelt
Bill Clinton	Labor History	Third Parties and Hopefuls
Democratic Items	Abraham Lincoln	Harry S Truman
Flashers	Local Items	Wendell Willkie
Gerald R. Ford	Ronald Reagan	Woman Suffrage

Some of the chapters have their own listings on the APIC web site.

Local Shows

Attending a political items show is one of the best ways to pick up new items, learn about collecting and meet other collectors. Shows are held throughout the year around the country. Here is a list of the approximate dates for each. For exact dates check the APIC web site, or one of the political collector newspapers, the *Political Bandwagon* or *Political Collector.*

February:	New York City	**April:**	Connecticut
	Chicago		Kentucky
	California		Wisconsin
	Florida	**May:**	Chicago
March:	Greensboro, NC		Michigan
	Indianapolis		New York City
	Washington, DC		New York State
	Des Moines, IA	**July:**	Hagerstown, MD

August: California   **November:**   Mid-Atlantic
September: Indianapolis   **December:**   St. Louis
October: Albany, NY
                       New England
                       New York City
                       Ohio

Related Organizations

The following are a few organizations of collectors of items which may include political campaign items. If you collect political items in one of these specialties you may find these organizations a good source of material.

American Matchcover
        Collecting Club
P. O. Box 18481
Ashville, NC 28814
http://www.matchcovers.com

American Philatelic Society
P. O. Box 8000
State College, PA
http://www.stamps.org

The Ephemera Society of America, Inc.
Membership Secretary
P. O. Box 95
Cazenovia, NY 13035-0095
http://www.ephemerasociety.org

National Knife Collectors Association
P. O. Box 21070
Chattanooga, TN 37424-0070
http://www.nationalknife.org

National Sheet Music Society
1597 Fair Park Ave.
Los Angeles, CA 90041
http://www.nsmsmusic.org

Newspaper Collectors'
        Society of America
6031 Winterset
Lansing, MI 48911

Paperweight Collectors' Assn.
274 Eastchester Dr. #117, PMB 130
High Point, NC 27262
http://www.paperweight.org/

Token and Medal Society
David Sklow
PO Box 76192
Ocala, FL 34481-0192
http://www.money.org/clubs/tams/

Books and Booklets

The most complete reference of political campaign items is a three volume set published by Ted Hake. The set was published over several years and the newer volumes include items missed in earlier volumes. Together the set covers over 12,000 different buttons. The original volumes were published in the 1970s, but there is a 2004 updated price guide.
        Encyclopedia of Political Buttons 1896-1972
        Encyclopedia of Political Buttons Book II 1920-1976
        Encyclopedia of Political Buttons III 1789-1916
        Unless you only collect pre-1896 items, you will need to get at least two volumes to cover any one election. That is because new items were discovered after the first volume was published.

For some candidates, collectors have cataloged the items into a single volume. If you plan to specialize in a single candidate these will be especially helpful.

John F. Kennedy:
The Campaign Buttons of John F. Kennedy
Bonnie Gardner & Harvey Goldberg
Self-published, 1980

J. F. K. Book II
Harvey Goldberg
Self-published, 1992

Robert F. Kennedy:
The Campaign Buttons of Robert F. Kennedy
Bonnie Gardner & Harvey Goldberg
Self-published, 1982

Richard M. Nixon:
The Political Collectibles of Richard Nixon
Eldon Almquist & Chris Crain
Self-published, 1989

Alton B. Parker:
Parker and Davis 1904
APIC, 1971

Adlai Stevenson:
Adlai E. Stevenson 1952-1956-1960
APIC, 1977

In addition to the above books, issues of the APIC *Keynoter* magazine have been devoted to specific candidates and include much useful information. Below is a list of the most recent articles on some popular candidates. Back issues are available through the APIC. A complete index is on their web site.

Adams	Fall 1993	Harrison	Fall 1981, Fall 1997
Bryan, W.J.	Spring 1980, Fall 2002	Hayes	Spring 2002
Buchanan	Summer 1994	Hoover	Winter 2003
Bush, G.H.W.	Winter 1987, Summer 1997	Hughes	Spring 1988
Bush, G.W.	Winter 2001	Jackson	Summer 1996
Clay	Fall 1997, Fall 1980	Johnson, L. B.	Spring 1993
Clinton	Winter 1993	Kennedy, J. F.	Winter 1980, Winter 2000, Summer 2002
Coolidge	Winter 1992		
Cox	Winter 1979, Fall, 1998	Kennedy, R.F.	Fall, 2003
Davis, Jeff.	Sum/Fall 1988	Landon	Autumn 1979
Davis, John	Fall/Winter 1983, Summer 2000, Fall 2001	Lincoln	Winter 1979, Spg/Sum 1990, Summer 1999
Debs	Mid-Year 1986, Spring, 1991, Winter 1994, Winter 1996	Lodge, H. C., Jr.	Winter 1991
		MacArthur	Spg/Sum 1989
Dewey	Spring 1983	McCarthy, E.	Winter 1989, Fall 2003
Dukakis	Summer 2002	McGovern	Winter 1982
Eisenhower	Winter 1986, Winter 2002	McKinley	Summer 1984, Fall 1984
Ferraro	Fall 2001	Nixon	Winter 2000, Spring 2003
Ford	Winter 2000	Pierce	Winter 1990, Summer 1996
Fremont	Summer 1985	Polk	Fall 1980
Goldwater	Summer 1982	Rockefeller	Winter 1990
Grant	Spring 2003	Roosevelt, F. D.	Spg./Sum. 1983
Hancock	Summer 1992	Roosevelt, T.	Summer 1981, Mid-Y 1986, 2004 No.1

Scott	Winter 1990	Truman	Summer, 1980
Smith	Winter 2003	Wallace, H.	Summer 1998, Summer 2003
Stevenson	Winter 2002	Willkie	Spring, 1986
Taft,	Spring, 1987, Fall 2002	Wilson	Spring, 1982
Tilden	Spring 2002		

For collectors who specialize in a certain type of item, rather than a candidate, there are several guides available. Some of these are out of print but copies may be located through a determined search.

Badges and Medalets:
*American Political Badges
    and Medalets 1789-1892*
Edmund B. Sullivan
Quarterman Publications, 1981

Cause items:
All for the Cause
William A. Sievert
Decoy Magazine, 1997

Canes:
*Canes in the United States/
    Illustrated Mementoes of
    American History, 1607-1953*
Catherine Dike
Cane Curiosa Press, 1994

Envelopes & letterhead:
*Presidential Campaign Illustrated
Envelopes and Letter Paper*
James W. Milgram
David G. Phillips, 1994

*Abraham Lincoln Illustrated Envelopes
and Letter Paper 1860-1865*
James W. Milgram
Northbrook Publishing, 1984

The Catalog of Union Civil War Patriotic Covers
William R. Weiss, Jr.
William R. Weiss, Jr., 1995

Postcards:
Political Postcards 1900-1980
Bernard Greenhouse
Postcard Press, 1980

Cloth items:
Threads of History
Herbert Ridgeway Collins
Smithsonian Institution Press 1979

Clothing Buttons:
Record of American Uniform and Historical Buttons
Alphaeus H. Albert
SCS & O'Donnell, 1997

Inaugural covers:
*Noble's Catalog of Presidential
Inaugural Covers*
        Edward Krohn
Noble Publishing, 1990

Convention tickets:
*Noble's Catalog and Price Guide of National
Political Convention Tickets and other
Convention Ephemera*
Edward Krohn
Noble Publishing, 1996

Stamps:
Political Campaign Stamps
Mark Warda
Krause Publications, 1998

Tabs:
Political Tabs
Robert Warren
Robert Warren, 1991

Periodicals

The Political Bandwagon
P. O. Box 348
Leola, PA 17540

The Political Collector
P. O. Box 5171
York, PA 17405

Auctions

The following dealers regularly hold mail-bid auctions of political items. There is usually a charge of $3 to $75 for their catalogs, however, some may send you a free sample if you say you saw their address in this book.

Al Anderson
P. O. Box 644
Troy, OH 45373
www.anderson-auction.com

Slater's Americana
5335 N. Tacoma Ave. #24
Indianapolis, IN 46220
www.slatersamericana.com

Cowan's
673 Wilmer Ave.
Cincinnati, OH 45226
www.historicamericana.com

The Rail Splitter
P O Box 275
New York, NY 10044

Tom French
P. O. Box 1755
Capitola, CA 95010

David Frent
P. O. Box 455
Oakhurst, NJ 07755

Hake's Americana
P. O. Box 1444
York, PA 17405
www.hakes.com

MastroNet Inc.
1515 W 22nd St. #125
Oak Brook, IL 60523
www.mastronet.com

HCA
3 Neptune Rd.
Poughkeepsie, NY 12601

David Quintin
P. O. Box 800861
Dallas, TX 75380

Historicana
P. O. Box 348
Leola, PA 17540

Dealers

The following dealers regularly or occasionally issue fixed price lists of political items for sale.

Be-In Buttons
PO Box 35593
Houston, TX 77235

Mort Berkowitz
1501 Broadway #1808
New York, NY 10036

Tom French
P. O. Box 65360
Tucson, AZ 85728

Fred Hester (Posters - $1 for list)
1615 Martha Ann Dr.
Maysville, KY 41056

Legacy Historical Antiques
3305 N. Swan Rd. PMB 109-423
Tucson, AZ 85712-1273

LBJ Museum
2313 Red River
Austin, TX 78705

Political Americana
1456 G Street NW
Washington, DC 20005

Mark Warda
P. O. Box 7
Clearwater, FL 33757

The following world wide web sites feature political items for sale:
http://www.permanentpromotions.com
http://www.political.com/buttons.html
http://www.politicalamericana.com
http://www.politicalparade.com
http://www.polamericana.com
http://www.galtpress.com
http://www.amres.com

Museums

Several museums have displays of political collectibles which are quite impressive. The best collections are at the following museums:

Museum of American Political Life
University of Hartford
Hartford, CT

National Museum of American History
Smithsonian Institution
Washington, DC

Cornell University Library
2B Carl A. Kroch Library
Ithaca, NY

In addition, all of our recent presidents have presidential libraries and museums, and many of these have displays of campaign items. The locations of those for our recent presidents are:

Herbert Hoover, West Branch, IA
Franklin D. Roosevelt, Hyde Park, NY
Harry S. Truman, Independence, MO
Dwight D. Eisenhower, Abilene, KS

John F. Kennedy, Boston, MA
Lyndon B. Johnson, Austin, TX
Richard M. Nixon, Yorba Linda, CA
Gerald Ford, Ann Arbor, MI
Jimmy Carter, Atlanta, GA and Plains, GA
Ronald Reagan, Simi Valley, CA
George Bush, College Station, TX
Bill Clinton, Little Rock, AR

Virtual Museums

John W. Davis Campaign Museum
http://www.johnwdavis.org

Inaugural items and political convention tickets
http://www.inaugurals.com

Shops

The following shops specialize in political items:

Capitol Stamp & Coin Co. Inc.
1001 Connecticut Ave. NW #745
Washington, DC 20036
202-296-0400

Mark's Americana
1725 Clearwater/Largo Rd. So.
Clearwater, FL 33756
727-581-8685
mark@warda.net
[moving to Lake Wales in 2005]

Political Americana
1331 Pennsylvania Ave., NW #100
Washington, DC 20004
800-333-4555

Political Americana
1331 Pennsylvania Ave., NW #100
Washington, DC 20004
800-333-4555

Presidential Coin & Antique Co.
6550-I Little River Tpk.
Alexandria, VA 22312
703-354-5454
JLevine968@aol.com

Insurance for Collectibles

Collectibles Insurance Agency
P. O. Box 1200
Westminster, MD 21158
1-888-837-9537
info@insurecollectibles.com
http://www.collectinsure.com

Association Insurance Administrators
P O Box 4389
Davidson, NC 28036
1.800.287.7127
Insure@AntiqueAndCollectible.com
http://www.AntiqueAndCollectible.com

Appendix 2: Presidential Nominees of All Parties 1789-2000

The following is a checklist of the presidential and vice-presidential candidates for all political parties for all elections since 1789. This list will help you determine what year a particular item is from and to which party the candidates belong. Five sources checked for vote totals all gave different figures. The highest total found in each case has been used. Numbers in parenthesis are the electoral votes.

1789
- Federalist (69)   George Washington
- Federalist (34)   John Adams
- Federalist (9)   John Jay
- Federalist (6)   Robert Hanson Harrison
- Federalist (6)   John Rutledge
- Federalist (4)   John Hancock
- Democratic-Republican (3)   George Clinton
- ? (2)   Samuel Huntington
- ? (2)   John Milton
- Federalist (1)   James Armstrong
- Federalist (1)   Benjamin Lincoln
- ? (1)   Edward Telfair

1792
- Federalist (132)   George Washington
- Federalist (77)   John Adams
- Democratic-Republican (50)   George Clinton
- Democratic-Republican (4)   Thomas Jefferson
- Democratic-Republican (1)   Aaron Burr

1796
- Federalist (71)   John Adams
- Democratic-Republican (68)   Thomas Jefferson
- Federalist (59)   Thomas Pinckney
- Democratic-Republican (30)   Aaron Burr
- Federalist (15)   Samuel Adams
- Federalist (11)   Oliver Ellsworth
- Democratic-Republican (7)   George Clinton
- Federalist (5)   John Jay
- Federalist (3)   James Iredell
- Democratic-Republican (2)   John Henry
- Federalist (2)   Samuel Johnson
- Federalist (2)   George Washington
- Federalist (1)   Charles Cotesworth Pinckney

1800
- Democratic-Republican (73)   Thomas Jefferson
- Democratic-Republican (73)   Aaron Burr
- Federalist (65)   John Adams
- Federalist (64)   Charles C. Pinckney
- Federalist (1)   John Jay

1804
☐ Democratic-Republican (162)   Thomas Jefferson
☐ Federalist (14)   Charles C. Pinckney

1808
☐ Democratic-Republican (122)   James Madison
☐ Federalist (47)   Charles C. Pinckney
☐ Democratic-Republican (6)   George Clinton

1812
☐ Democratic-Republican (128)   James Madison John Langdon
☐ Federalist (89)   Dewitt Clinton Jared Ingersoll

1816
☐ Democratic-Republican (183)   James Monroe Daniel D. Tompkins
☐ Federalist (33)   Rufus King John Howard

1820
☐ Democratic-Republican (231)   James Monroe Daniel D. Tompkins
☐ Democratic-Republican (1)   John Quincy Adams

1824
☐ Democratic-Republican (99)   Andrew Jackson John C. Calhoun   153,544
☐ Democratic-Republican (84)   John Quincy Adams John C. Calhoun   108,740
☐ Democratic-Republican (41)   William Harris Crawford Albert Gallatin 47,136
☐ Democratic-Republican (37)   Henry Clay John C. Calhoun   46,618

1828
☐ Democrat (178)   Andrew Jackson John C. Calhoun   647,286
☐ National Republican (83)   John Quincy Adams Richard Rush   508,064

1832
☐ Democrat (219)   Andrew Jackson Martin Van Buren   687,502
☐ National Republican (49)   Henry Clay John Sergeant   530,189
☐ Independent Democrats (11)   John Floyd Henry Lee
☐ Anti-Masonic (7)   William Wirt Amos Ellmaker   101,051

1836
☐ Democrat (170)   Martin Van Buren Richard M. Johnson   762,678
☐ Anti-Masonic/Whig (73)   William Henry Harrison Francis Granger 549,508
☐ Whig (26)   Hugh L. White John Tyler   145,352
☐ Whig (14)   Daniel Webster Francis Granger   41,287
☐ Independent/Whig (11)   Willie Person Mangum

1840
☐ Whig (234)   William Henry Harrison John Tyler   1,275,016
☐ Democratic (60)   Martin Van Buren [varied by state]   1,129,102
☐ Liberty/Prohibition   James G. Birney Thomas Earle   7,069

1844
☐ Democratic (170)   James K. Polk George M. Dallas   1,337,243
☐ Whig (105)   Henry Clay Theodore Frelinghuysen   1,299,062
☐ Liberty/Prohibition   James G. Birney Thomas Morris   62,300

1848
☐ Whig (163)   Zachary Taylor Millard Fillmore   1,360,099
☐ Democratic (127)   Lewis Cass William Butler   1,220,544
☐ Free Soil   Martin Van Buren Charles F. Adams   291,263
☐ National Liberty   Gerrit Smith Charles C. Foote   2,733

1852
☐ Democratic (254)   Franklin Pierce William King   1,601,747
☐ Whig (42)   Winfield Scott William A. Graham   1,386,580
☐ Free Soil   John Parker Hale George W. Julian   155,285
☐ Whig   Daniel Webster   7,407
☐ American   James E. Broome   2,666
☐ Southern Rights   George Michael Troop   2,300
☐ National Liberty   Gerrit Smith   72

1856
☐ Democratic (174)   James Buchanan John Breckenridge   1,838,169
☐ Republican (114)   John C. Fremont William Dayton   1,341,264
☐ American Know Nothing/Whig   Millard Fillmore A. J. Donelson   874,534
☐ Land Reform   Gerrit Smith   484
☐ North American   Nathaniel P. Banks William F. Johnson

1860
☐ Republican (180)   Abraham Lincoln Hannibal Hamlin   1,867,198
☐ Democrat (72)   John C. Breckinridge Joseph Lane   854,248
☐ Constitutional Union (39)   John Bell Edward Everett   591,658
☐ Democrat (12)   Stephen A. Douglas H. V. Johnson   1,379,434

1864
☐ Republican (212)   Abraham Lincoln Andrew Johnson   2,219,362
☐ Democrat (21)   George B. McClellan G. H. Pendleton   1,805,063
☐ Independent Republican   John C. Fremont John Cochrane

1868
☐ Republican (214)   Ulysses S. Grant Henry Wilson   3,013,313
☐ Democrat (80)   Horatio, Seymour Francis Blair Jr.   2,703,933

1872
☐ Republican (286)   Ulysses S. Grant Henry Wilson   3,597,375
☐ Democrat (3) (died before electoral vote) Horace Greeley B. Gratz Brown   2,833,711
☐ Democrat (42)   Thomas Hendricks George Julian
☐ Democrat (18)   B. Gratz Brown
☐ Democrat (2)   Charles Jenkins
☐ Democrat (1)   David Davis Joel Parker
☐ Straight-out Democratic   Charles O Conor Charles Francis Adams   29,489
☐ Prohibition   James Black John Russell   5,608
☐ Independent Liberal Republican   William S. Groesbeck Frederick L. Olmstead
☐ People s/Equal Rights   Victoria C. Woodhull Frederick Douglass

1876
☐ Repepublican (185)   Rutherford B. Hayes William Wheeler   4,035,924
☐ Democrat (184)   Samuel J. Tilden Thomas Hendricks   4,287,670
☐ Greenback   Peter Cooper Samuel Cary   81,737
☐ Prohibition   Green Clay Smith Gideon Tabor Stewart   6,743
☐ American National   James B. Walker Donald Kirkpatrick   459

1880

☐ Republican (214)	James A. Garfield Chester A. Arthur	4,454,433
☐ Democrat (155)	Winfield S. Hancock William English	4,444,976
☐ Greenback	James B. Weaver B. J. Chambers	308,649
☐ Prohibition	Neal Dow Henry A. Thompson	10,305
☐ American	John W. Phelps Samuel C. Pomeroy	700

1884

☐ Democrat (219)	Grover Cleveland Thomas Hendricks	4,875,971
☐ Republican (182)	James G. Blaine John Logan	4,852,234
☐ Greenback/Anti-Monopoly	Benjamin Butler A.M. West	175,370
☐ Prohibition	John St. John William Daniel	150,369
☐ Equal Rights	Belva A. B. Lockwood Marietta L. B. Stow	4,149
☐ American Prohibition	Samuel C. Pomeroy John A. Conant	

1888

☐ Republican (233)	Benjamin Harrison Levi P. Morton	5,444,337
☐ Democratic (168)	Grover Cleveland Allen G. Thurman	5,540,309
☐ Prohibition	Clinton B. Fisk John A. Brooks	249,506
☐ Union Labor	Alson J. Streeter Charles E. Cunningham	146,935
☐ United Labor	Robert H. Cowdrey William H. T. Wakefield	2,818
☐ American	James L. Curtis Peter Dinwiddie Wigginton	1,612
☐ Equal Rights	Belva A. B. Lockwood Alfred H. Love	
☐ Industrial Reform	Albert E. Redstone John Colvin	

1892

☐ Democratic (277)	Grover Cleveland Adlai E. Stevenson	5,556,918
☐ Republican (145)	Benjamin Harrison Whitelaw Reid	5,176,108
☐ Peoples (22)	James Baird Weaver James G. Field	1,041,028
☐ Prohibition	John Bidwell James B. Cranfill	264,133
☐ Socialist-Labor	Simon Wing Charles H. Matchett	21,512

1896

☐ Republican (271)	William McKinley—Garret A. Hobart	7,113,734
☐ Dem./People's Pop.(176)	William J. Bryan—Arthur Sewall	6,511,495
☐ Gold Democratic	John M. Palmer—Simon B. Buckner	135,456
☐ Prohibition	Joshua Levering—Hale Johnson	132,007
☐ Socialist Labor	Charles H. Matchett—Matthew Maguire	36,475
☐ National Prohibition	Charles E. Bentley—James H. Southgate	19,363
☐ Silver	William J. Bryan—Arthur Sewall	

1900

☐ Republican (292)	William McKinley—Theodore Roosevelt	7,219,828
☐ Democratic (155)	William J. Bryan—Adlai E. Stevenson	6,358,345
☐ Prohibition	John G. Woolley—Henry B. Metcalf	210,200
☐ Social Dem. of America	Eugene V. Debs—Job Harriman	95,744
☐ Populist	Wharton Barker—Ignatious Donnelly	50,605
☐ Socialist-Labor	Joseph F. Malloney—Valentine Remmel	40,900
☐ Union Reform	Seth H. Ellis—Samuel Nicholson	5,698
☐ United Christian	Jonah F. R. Leonard—David H. Martin	5,500
☐ National	Donelson Caffery—Archibald M. Howe	
☐ People's/Fusionists	William J. Bryan—Adlai E. Stevenson	
☐ Silver Republican	William J. Bryan—Adlai E. Stevenson	
☐ Social Dem. of U.S.A.	Job Harriman—Maximilian S. Hayes	

1904
- ☐ Republican (336) · Theodore Roosevelt—Charles W. Fairbanks · 7,628,831
- ☐ Democratic (140) · Alton B. Parker—Henry G. Davis · 5,084,898
- ☐ Socialist/Socialist Dem. · Eugene V. Debs—Benjamin Hanford · 402,714
- ☐ Prohibition · Silas C. Swallow—George W. Carroll · 259,163
- ☐ Populist · Thomas E. Watson—Thomas H. Tibbles · 117,183
- ☐ Socialist Labor · Charles H. Corregan—William W. Cox · 33,737
- ☐ Continental · Austin Holcomb—A. King · 1,000
- ☐ National Liberal/Colored · George E. Taylor—W. C. Payne

1908
- ☐ Republican (321) · William H. Taft—James S. Sherman · 7,678,908
- ☐ Democratic (162) · William J. Bryan—John W. Kern · 6,412,294
- ☐ Socialist · Eugene V. Debs—Benjamin Hanford · 420,793
- ☐ Prohibition · Eugene W. Chafin—Aaron S. Watkins · 253,840
- ☐ Independence · Thomas L. Hisgen—John T. Graves · 82,872
- ☐ Populist · Thomas E. Watson—Samuel W. Williams · 29,100
- ☐ Socialist Labor · August Gillhaus—Donald L. Munro · 14,021
- ☐ United Christian · Daniel B. Turner—Lorenzo S. Coffin · 500

1912
- ☐ Democratic (435) · T. Woodrow Wilson—Thomas R. Marshall · 6,296,547
- ☐ Progressive/Bull Moose (88) · Theodore Roosevelt—Hiram W. Johnson · 4,119,538
- ☐ Republican (8) · William H. Taft—James S. Sherman · 3,486,720
- ☐ Socialist · Eugene V. Debs—Emil Seidel · 901,873
- ☐ Prohibition · Eugene W. Chafin—Aaron S. Watkins · 207,972
- ☐ Socialist Labor · Arthur E. Reimer—August Gillhaus · 29,374

1916
- ☐ Democratic (277) · T. Woodrow Wilson—Thomas R. Marshall · 9,129,606
- ☐ Republican (254) · Charles E. Hughes—Charles W. Fairbanks · 8,546,789
- ☐ Socialist · Allan L. Benson—George R. Kirkpatrick · 590,322
- ☐ Prohibition · J. Frank Hanly—Ira Landrith · 221,030
- ☐ Progressive · Theodore Roosevelt—John M. Parker · 35,054
- ☐ Socialist Labor · Arthur E. Reimer—Caleb Harrison · 15,284
- ☐ American · William Sulzer—I.G. Pollard

1920
- ☐ Republican (404) · Warren G. Harding—Calvin Coolidge · 16,153,115
- ☐ Democratic (127) · James M. Cox—Franklin D. Roosevelt · 9,147,353
- ☐ Socialist · Eugene V. Debs—Seymour Stedman · 919,799
- ☐ Farmer Labor · Parley P. Christensen—Maximilian S. Hayes · 265,411
- ☐ Prohibition · Aaron S. Watkins—David L. Colvin · 189,408
- ☐ American · James E. Ferguson · 48,000
- ☐ Socialist Labor · William W. Cox—August Gillhaus · 31,715
- ☐ Single Tax · Robert C. Macauley—Richard C. Barnum · 5,837

1924
- ☐ Republican (382) · J. Calvin Coolidge—Charles G. Dawes · 15,725,016
- ☐ Democratic (136) · John W. Davis—Charles W. Bryan · 8,386,704
- ☐ Progressive/Socialist (13) · Robert M. La Follette—Burton K. Wheeler · 4,832,532
- ☐ Prohibition · Herman P. Faris—Marie C. Brehm · 57,551
- ☐ Socialist Labor · Frank T. Johns—Verne L. Reynolds · 38,958
- ☐ Communist/Workers · William Z. Foster—Benjamin Gitlow · 36,386

☐ American	Gilbert O. Nations—Charles H. Randall	24,340
☐ Commonwealth Land	William J. Wallace—John C. Lincoln	2,948
☐ Farmer Labor	William Z. Foster—Benjamin Gitlow	
☐ National Independent	John Zahnd—Roy M. Harrop	
☐ People's Progressive	Robert R. Pointer—Roy M. Harrop	

1928

☐ Republican (444)	Hebert C. Hoover—Charles Curtis	21,437,277
☐ Democratic (87)	Alfred E. Smith—Joseph T. Robinson	15,016,443
☐ Socialist	Norman M. Thomas—James H. Maurer	267,835
☐ Communist/Workers	William Z. Foster—Benjamin Gitlow	48,770
☐ Socialist Labor	Verne L. Reynolds—Jeremiah D. Crowley	21,603
☐ Prohibition	William F. Varney—James A. Edgerton	20,106
☐ Farmer Labor	Frank E. Webb—LeRoy Tillman	6,390
☐ National Independent	John Zahnd—Wesley H. Bennington	6,390
☐ National Progressive	Dr. Henry Hoffman—Jane Addams	

1932

☐ Democratic (472)	Franklin D. Roosevelt—James N. Garner	22,829,501
☐ Republican (59)	Herbert C. Hoover—Charles Curtis	15,761,841
☐ Socialist	Norman M. Thomas—John H. Maurer	884,781
☐ Communist/Workers	William Z. Foster—James W. Ford	103,253
☐ Prohibition	William D. Upshaw—Frank S. Regan	81,872
☐ Liberty	William H. Harvey—Frank B. Hemenway	53,425
☐ Socialist Labor	Verne L. Reynolds—John W. Aiken	34,043
☐ Farmer Labor	Jacob S. Coxey—Julius J. Reiter	7,431
☐ National Independent	John Zahnd—Florence Garvin	1,645
☐ Jobless/Blue Shirts	James R. Cox—Victor C. Tisdal	740
☐ Liberty And Unity	Frank E. Webb—Andrae Nordskog	

1936

☐ Democratic (523)	Franklin D. Roosevelt—John N. Garner	27,757,333
☐ Republican (8)	Alfred M. Landon—Frank Knox	16,684,231
☐ Union	William Lemke—Thomas C. O'Brien	892,267
☐ Socialist	Norman M. Thomas—George A. Nelson	187,833
☐ Communist	Earl R. Browder—James W. Ford	80,171
☐ Prohibition	D. Leigh Colvin—Claude A. Watson	37,847
☐ Socialist Labor	John W. Aiken—Emil F. Teichert	12,829
☐ Greenback	John Zahnd—Florence Garvin	
☐ Christian	William D. Pelley	1,598

1940

☐ Demoratic (449)	Fanklin D. Roosevelt—Henry A. Wallace	27,313,041
☐ Republican (82)	Wendell L. Willkie—Charles L. McNary	22,348,480
☐ Socialist	Norman M. Thomas—Maynard C. Krueger	116,410
☐ Prohibition	Roger W. Babson—Edgar V. Moorman	58,708
☐ Communist	Earl R. Browder—James W. Ford	46,251
☐ Socialist Labor	John W. Aiken—Aaron M. Orange	14,892
☐ Independent	Alfred Knutson	545
☐ Greenback	John Zahnd—James E. Yates	

1944

☐ Democratic (432)	Franklin D. Roosevelt—Harry S. Truman	25,612,610
☐ Republican (99)	Thomas E. Dewey—John W. Bricker	22,017,617
☐ Socialist	Norman M. Thomas—Darlington Hoopes	80,518

☐ Prohibition   Claude A. Watson—Andrew Johnson   74,779
☐ Socialist Labor   Edward A. Teichert—Arla A. Albaugh   45,336
☐ America First   Gerald L. K. Smith—Harry A. Romer   1,780
☐ Greenback   Leo C. Donnelly—Frank Jeffries
☐ Texas Regulars   135,444

1948
☐ Democratic/Liberal (304)   Harry S. Truman—Alben W. Barkley   24,179,345
☐ Republican (189)   Thomas E. Dewey—Earl Warren   21,991,291
☐ States' Rts. (Dixiecrats) (38) J. Strom Thurmond—Fielding L. Wright   1,176,125
☐ Progressive   Henry A. Wallace—Glen H. Taylor   1,157,326
☐ Socialist   Norman M. Thomas—Tucker P. Smith   139,572
☐ Prohibition   Claude A. Watson—Dale H. Learn   103,900
☐ Socialist Labor   Edward A. Teichert—Stephen Emery   29,272
☐ Socialist Workers   Farrell Dobbs—Grace Carlson   13,613
☐ Christian Nationalist   Gerald L. K. Smith—Harry A. Romer   42
☐ Greenback   John G. Scott—Granville B. Leeke   6
☐ American Vegetarian   John Maxwell—Symon Gould   4
☐ Communist   Henry A. Wallace—Glen H. Taylor

1952
☐ Republican (442)   Dwight D. Eisenhower—Richard M. Nixon 33,936,252
☐ Democratic (89)   Adlai E. Stevenson—John J. Sparkman   27,314,992
☐ Progressive/American Labor Vincent W. Hallinan—Charlotta A. Bass   140,138
☐ Prohibition   Stuart Hamblen—Enoch A. Holtwick   72,949
☐ Socialist Labor   Eric Hass—Stephen Emery   30,376
☐ Socialist   Darlington Hoopes—Samuel H. Friedman   20,203
☐ Constitution   Douglas A. MacArthur—Jack B. Tenny   17,205
☐ Socialist Workers   Farrell Dobbs—Myra T. Weiss   10,312
☐ Poor Man's Party   Henry J. Krajewski—Frank Jenkins   4,203
☐ Constitution   Douglas A. MacArthur—Harry F. Byrd   2,911
☐ America First   Douglas A. MacArthur—Harry F. Byrd   233
☐ Constitution Of California Douglas A. MacArthur—Vivien Kellems   178
☐ American Vegetarian   Daniel J. Murphy—Symon Gould
☐ Greenback   Frederick C. Proehl—J. Edward Bedell
☐ Communist   Vincent W. Hallinan—Charlotta A. Bass
☐ Theocratic/Church Of God   Homer A. Tomlinson—Willie I. Bass
☐ Washington Peace   Ellen L. Jensen

1956
☐ Republican (457)   Dwight D. Eisenhower—Richard M. Nixon 35,590,472
☐ Democratic/Liberal (74)   Adlai E. Stevenson—Estes Kefauver   26,028,887
☐ Independent   T. Coleman Andrews—Thomas H. Werdel   275,915
☐ States' Rights—Kentucky   Harry F. Byrd—William E. Jenner   134,157
☐ Soc. Labor/Indust. Govt.   Eric Hass—Georgia Cozzini   44,450
☐ Prohibition   Enoch A. Holtwick—Edwin M. Cooper   41,937
☐ Texas Constitution   William E. Jenner—J. Bracken Lee   30,999
☐ Socialist Workers   Farrell Dobbs—Myra T. Weiss   8,148
☐ Black & Tan Grand Old Party Dwight D. Eisenhower—Richard M. Nixon   4,313
☐ Socialist   Darlington Hoopes—Samuel H. Friedman   2,192
☐ American Third Party   Henry B. Krajewski—Anna M. Yezo   1,892
☐ Christian Nationalist   Gerald L. K. Smith—Charles F. Robertson   8
☐ Constitution   T. Coleman Andrews—Thomas H. Werdel
☐ States' Rights   Harry F. Byrd—Thomas H. Werdel

☐ American Vegetarian   Herbert M. Shelton—Symon Gould
☐ Greenback   Frederick C. Proehl—Edward K. Meador
☐ Pioneer   William Langer—Burr McCloskey
☐ South Carolinians for Independent Electors   Harry F. Byrd

1960

☐ Democratic (330)	John F. Kennedy—Lyndon B. Johnson	34,227,096
☐ Republican (223)	Richard M. Nixon—Henry Cabot Lodge	34,108,647
☐ Independent (15)	Harry F. Byrd	462,575
☐ National States' Rights	Orval E. Faubus—John G. Crommelin	214,549
☐ Soc. Labor/Industrial Govt.	Eric Hass—George Cozzini	47,522
☐ Prohibition	Rutherford L. Decker—E. Harold Munn	46,220
☐ Socialist Workers	Farrell Dobbs—Myra T. Weiss	40,175
☐ Constitution of Texas	Charles L. Sullivan—Merritt B. Curtis	18,169
☐ Conserv. of New Jersey	J. Bracken Lee—Kent H. Courtney	8,708
☐ Virginia Conservative	C. Benton Coiner—Edward J. Silverman	4,204
☐ Tax Cut	Lar (Lawrence J. S.) Daly—Bryan M. Miller	1,767
☐ Ind. Afro-American Unity	Clennon King—Reginald Carter	1,485
☐ Constitution	Merritt B. Curtis—Bryan M. Miller	1,401
☐ Liberal	John F. Kennedy—Lyndon B. Johnson	
☐ American Third	Henry B. Krajewski	
☐ American Vegetarian	Symon Gould—Christopher Gian-Cursio	
☐ Greenback	Whitney H. Slocomb—Edward K. Meador	
☐ Mankind's Assembly	Lewis Bertrand	
☐ Outer Space	Gabriel Green—Addison Brown	
☐ Rocking Chair	Connie Watts—Ralph Raper	
☐ Theocratic/Church Of God	Homer A. Tomlinson—Raymond L. Teague	
☐ Independent	Jack Moore	
☐ Independent	William L. Smith	
☐ Independent	Agnes Waters	

1964

☐ Democratic (486)	Lyndon B. Johnson—Hubert H. Humphrey	43,129,566
☐ Republican (82)	Barry M. Goldwater—William Miller	27,178,188
☐ Liberal	Lyndon B. Johnson—Hubert H. Humphrey	342,432
☐ Alabama Unpledged Elec.		210,732
☐ Socialist Labor	Eric Hass—Henning Blomen	45,219
☐ Socialist Workers	Clifton DeBerry—Edward Shaw	32,720
☐ Prohibition	E. Harold Munn—Mark Shaw	23,267
☐ National States' Rights	John Kasper—J. B. Stoner	6,953
☐ Constitution	Joseph B. Lightburn—Theodore Billings	5,090
☐ Theocratic	Homer A. Tomlinson—William Rogers	20
☐ Universal Party	James Hensley—John Hopkins	19
☐ Peace	Mirhan Ask	10
☐ America First	Lar (Lawrence J. S.) Daly	8
☐ Car And Driver	Dan Gurney	6
☐ Independent States' Rights	T. Coleman Andrews	
☐ Best Party	Yette Bronstein	
☐ American	Louis E. Jaeckel	
☐ American Nazi	George L. Rockwell	
☐ Metropolitan	Wilbur Huckle—Marv Throneberry	
☐ National Tax Savers	D. X. B. Schwartz	
☐ Poor Man's	Henry B. Krajewski—Ann Yezo	
☐ United	Grant Van Tilborg—Harold Putnam	
☐ United Nations	Emil Matalik	
☐ Vegetarian	Symon Gould—Abram Wolfson	

1968

☐ Republican (301)	Richard M. Nixon—Spiro Agnew	31,785,480
☐ Democratic (191)	Hubert H. Humphrey—Edmund Muskie	31,275,166
☐ American Independent (46)	George C. Wallace—Curtis LeMay	9,906,473
☐ Liberal	Hubert H. Humphrey—Edmund Muskie	311,622
☐ Socialist Labor	Henning A. Blomen—George Taylor	52,594
☐ Freedom And Peace	Dick Gregory—D. Frost, M. Lane, B. Spock	47,133
☐ Socialist Workers	Fred Halstead—Paul Boutelle	41,389
☐ Peace And Freedom	Eldridge Cleaver—(various)	36,565
☐ New Party	Eugene J. McCarthy—John Lindsey	27,067
☐ Prohibition	E. Harold Munn—Rolland Fisher	15,123
☐ People's Constitutional	Ventura Chavez—Adelicio Moya	1,519
☐ Communist	Charlene Mitchell—Michael Zagarell	1,075
☐ Universal	James Hensley—Roscoe MacKenna	142
☐ Constitution	Richard K. Troxell—Merl Thayer	34
☐ Berkley Defense Group	Kent M. Soeters—James Powers	17
☐ America First	Lar (Lawrence J. S.) Daly	
☐ Theocratic	Homer A. Tomlinson—W. B. McKenzie	

1972

☐ Republican (520)	Richard M. Nixon—Spiro Agnew	47,169,911
☐ Democratic (17)	George S. McGovern—Sargent Shriver	29,170,383
☐ American	John G. Schmitz—Thomas Anderson	1,107,083
☐ Liberal	George McGovern—Sargent Shriver	183,128
☐ Socialist Workers	Linda Jenness—Andrew Pulley	97,295
☐ People's	Benjamin Spock—Julius Hobson	78,889
☐ Socialist Labor	Louis Fisher—Genevieve Gunderson	53,815
☐ Communist	Gus Hall—Jarvis Tyner	25,621
☐ Socialist Workers	Evelyn Reed	13,878
☐ Prohibition	E. Harold Munn—Marshall Uncapher	13,505
☐ Libertarian (1)	John Hospers—Theodora Nathan	3,697
☐ America First	John V. Mahalchik—Irving Homer	1,743
☐ Independent	Edward Wallace—Robert Mess	460
☐ Universal	Gabriel Green—Daniel Fry	220

1976

☐ Democratic (297)	James E. Carter—Walter Mondale	40,830,763
☐ Republican (241)	Gerald R. Ford—Robert Dole	39,147,793
☐ Independent	Eugene J. McCarthy	756,691
☐ Libertarian	Roger MacBride—David Bergland	173,011
☐ American Independent	Lester G. Maddox—William Dyke	170,780
☐ American	Thomas J. Anderson—Rufus Shackleford	160,773
☐ Socialist Workers	Peter Camejo—Willie Mae Reid	91,314
☐ Communist	Gus Hall—Jarvis Tyner	59,114
☐ People's Party	Margaret Wright—Benjamin Spock	49,024
☐ U.S. Labor	Lyndon H. LaRouche, Jr.—R. W. Evans	40,045
☐ Prohibition	Benjamin C. Bubar—Earl Dodge	15,934
☐ Socialist Labor	Jules Levin—Constance Blomen	9,616
☐ Socialist	Frank P. Zeidler—J. Quinn Brisben	6,038
☐ Restoration	Ernest L. Miller—Roy Eddy	361
☐ United American	Frank Taylor—Henry Swan	36
☐ Constitutional	Paul Cunningham	
☐ Independent	Billy Joe Clegg—Auburn L. Packwood	
☐ Independent	F. D. Kirkpatrick	

☐ Independent   Donald Jackson
☐ Independent   Kenyon Knourek
☐ Independent   Ellen McCormack
☐ Independent   Pat Patton
☐ Independent   Chief Burning Wood—Austin Burton

1980

☐ Republican (489)	Ronald W. Reagan—George H. W. Bush	43,904,153
☐ Democratic (49)	James E. Carter—Walter Mondale	35,483,883
☐ National Unity Campaign	John B. Anderson—Patrick Lucey	5,720,060
☐ Libertarian	Edward Clark—David Koch	921,299
☐ Citizens	Barry Commoner—Ladonna Harris	234,294
☐ Communist	Gus Hall—Angela Davis	45,954
☐ American Independent	John R. Rarick—Eileen Shearer	41,268
☐ Socialist Workers	Clifton DeBerry—Matilde Zimmerman	40,145
☐ Right To Life	Ellen McCormack—Carroll Driscoll	32,327
☐ Peace And Freedom	Maureen Smith—Elizabeth Barron	18,117
☐ Workers World	Deirdre Griswold—Larry Holmes	13,300
☐ Statesman (Prohibition)	Benjamin C. Bubar—Earl Dodge	7,212
☐ Socialist	David McReynolds—Diane Drufenbrock	6,898
☐ American	Percy L. Greaves—Frank Varnum	6,647
☐ Socialist Workers	Andrew Pulley—Matilde Zimmerman	6,272
☐ Socialist Workers	Richard Congress—Matilde Zimmerman	4,029
☐ Middle Class	Kurt Lynen—Harry Kieve	3,694
☐ Down With Lawyers	Bill Gahres—J. F. Loghlin	1,718
☐ American	Frank W. Shelton—George Jackson	1,555
☐ Independent	Martin E. Wendelken	923
☐ Natural Peoples League	Harley McLain—Jewelie Goeller	296
☐ Independent	Luther Wilson	
☐ Write-Ins	(Various)	16,921

1984

☐ Republican (525)	Ronald W. Reagan—George H. W. Bush	54,455,075
☐ Democratic (13)	Walter F. Mondale—Geraldine Ferraro	37,577,185
☐ Libertarian	David Bergland—Jim Lewis	228,314
☐ Independent	Lyndon H. LaRouche, Jr.—Billy Davis	78,807
☐ Citizens	Sonia Johnson—Richard Walton	72,200
☐ Populist	Bob Richards—Maureen Kennedy Salaman	66,336
☐ Independent Alliance	Dennis L. Serrette—Nancy Ross	46,868
☐ Communist	Gus Hall—Angela Davis	36,386
☐ Socialist Workers	Mel Mason—Andrea Gonzalez	24,706
☐ Workers World	Larry Holmes—Gloria Lariva	15,329
☐ American	Delmar Davis—Traves Brownlee	13,161
☐ Workers League	Ed Winn—E. Berganzi, J. Brust, H. Halyard	10,801
☐ Prohibition	Earl F. Dodge—Warren C. Martin	4,242
☐ Workers World	Gabrielle Holmes—Milton Vera	2,656
☐ National Unity Party of Kentucky	John B. Anderson	1,486
☐ Big Deal	Gerald Baker	892
☐ United Sovereign Citizens	Arthur J. Lowery	825
☐ Independent	Neil K. Filoa	
☐ Independent	William J. Dupont	

1988

☐ Republican (426)	George H. W. Bush—Dan Quayle	48,886,097
☐ Democratic (111)	Michael S. Dukakis—Lloyd Bentsen	41,809,074
☐ Libertarian	Ron Paul—Andre V. Marrou	432,179
☐ New Alliance	Lenora B. Fulani—Joyce Dattner (and others)	217,219
☐ Populist	David E. Duke—Floyd Parker	47,047
☐ Consumer	Eugene J. McCarthy—Florence Rice	30,905
☐ American Independent	James C. Griffin—Charles "Chuck" Morsa	27,818
☐ Natl. Economic Recovery	Lyndon H. LaRouche, Jr.	25,562
☐ Right to Life	William A. Marra—John Andrews	20,504
☐ Workers League	Ed Winn—Barry Porster	18,693
☐ Socialist Workers	James Warren—Kathleen Mickells	15,604
☐ Peace and Freedom	Herbert Lewis—Emma Mar	10,370
☐ Prohibition	Earl F. Dodge—George Ormsby	8,002
☐ Workers World	Larry Holmes—Gloria LaRiva	7,846
☐ Socialist	Willa Kenoyer—Ron Ehrenreich	3,882
☐ American	Delmar Dennis—Earl Jeppson	3,476
☐ Grassroots	Jack E. Herer	1,949
☐ Independent	Louie G. Youngkeit	372
☐ Third World Assembly	John G. Martin	236
☐ Independent	Neil K. Filoa	
☐ Independent	Jack Moore	

1992

☐ Democratic (370)	William J. Clinton—Albert Gore, Jr.	44,909,326
☐ Republican (168)	George H. W. Bush—Dan Quayle	38,117,331
☐ Independent	H. Ross Perot—James Stockdale	19,714,657
☐ Libertarian	Andre V. Marrou—Nancy Lord	291,627
☐ Populist	James " Bo" Gritz—Cy Minette	107,014
☐ New Alliance	Lenora B. Fulani—Elizabeth Munz	73,714
☐ U. S. Taxpayers	Howard Phillips—Gen. Aldion Knight	43,434
☐ Natural Law	John Hagelin—Dr. Mike Tompkins	39,179
☐ Peace & Freedom	Ron Daniels—Asiba Tupahache	27,961
☐ Economic Recovery	Lyndon H. LaRouche, Jr.—James Bevel (and others)	26,333
☐ Socialist Workers	James Warren—Estelle DeDate	23,096
☐ Independent	Drew Bradford	4,749
☐ Grassroots	Jack E. Herer—Derrick P. Grimmer	3,875
☐ Socialist	J. Quinn Brisben—William D. Edwards*	3,057
☐ Workers League	Helen Halyard—Fred Mazelis	3,050
☐ Take Back America	John Yiamouyiannas—Allen C. McCone	2,199
☐ Independent	Delbert L. Ehlers—Rick Wendt	1,149
☐ Prohibition	Earl F. Dodge—George Ormsby	961
☐ Apathy	Jim Boren—Bill Wiedman	956
☐ Third	Eugene A. Hem—JoanneRolland	405
☐ Looking Back	Isabell Masters—Walter Masters	339
☐ American	Robert J. Smith—Doris Feimer	292
☐ Workers World	Gloria LaRiva—Larry Holmes	181
☐ Queer Nation	Terence Smith—Joan Jett Blakk	

*Edwards died prior to the election and was replaced by Barbara Garson. Buttons for both candidates were made.

1996

☐ Democratic (379)	William. J. Clinton—Albert Gore, Jr.	47,402,357
☐ Republican (159)	Robert Dole—Jack Kemp	39,198,755
☐ Reform	H. Ross Perot—Pat Choate	8,085,403
☐ Green	Ralph Nader— Winona LaDuke	685,128
☐ Libertarian	Harry Browne—Jo Jorgensen	485,795
☐ U.S. Taxpayers	Howard Phillips—Herbert Titus	182,820
☐ Natural Law	John Hagelin—Mike Tompkins	113,671
☐ Workers World	Monica Moorehead—Gloria LaRiva	29,083
☐ Peace and Freedom	Marcia Feinland—Kate McClatchy	25,332
☐ Independent	Charles Collins—Rosemary Guimarra	8,952
☐ Socialist Workers	James Harris—Laura Garza	8,476
☐ None of the above (Nevada)		5,608
☐ Grass Roots	Dennis Peron—Arlin Troutt	5,378
☐ Socialist	Mary Hollis—Eric T. Chester	4,766
☐ Socialist Equality	Jerome White—Fred Mazelis	2,438
☐ American	Diane Templin—Gary VanHorn	1,847
☐ Prohibition	Earl Dodge—Rachel B. Kelly	1,298
☐ Independent of Utah	Peter Crane—Connie Chandler	1,101
☐ America First	Justice Ralph Forbes—Pro-Life Anderson	932
☐ Independent Grassroots	John Birrenbach	787
☐ Looking Back	Isabell Masters—Shirley Jean Masters	752
☐ AIDS Cure	Steve Michael	408
☐ Queer Nation	Joan Jett Blakk	

2000

☐ Republican (270)	George W. Bush—Richard B. Cheney	50,456,002
☐ Democratic (266)	Albert Gore, Jr.—Joseph Lieberman	50,999,897
☐ Green	Ralph Nader—Winona LaDuke	2,882,955
☐ Reform	Patrick Buchanan—Ezola Foster	448,895
☐ Libertarian	Harry Browne—Art Olivier	384,431
☐ Constitution	Howard Phillips—Curt Frazier	98,020
☐ Natural Law/Reform	John Hagelin—Nat Goldhaber	83,714
☐ Socialist Workers	James Harris—Maggie Trowe	7,378
☐ Socialist	David Reynolds—Mary Cal Hollis	5,602
☐ Libertarian (Arizona)	L. Neil Smith— Vin Suprynowicz	5,775
☐ Workers World	Monica Moorehead—Gloria LaRiva	4,795
☐ None of these Candidates (Nevada)		3,315
☐ Independent	Cathy Gordon Brown—Sabrina R. Allen	1,606
☐ Grassroots	Denny Lane—Dale Wilkinson	1,044
☐ Independent	Randall Venson—Gene Kelly	535
☐ Prohibition	Earl Dodge—Dean Watkins	208
☐ Independent	Louie Youngkeit—Robert L. Beck	161
☐ American Party	Don Rogers—Al Moore	
☐ Progressive/Bull Moose Party	Thomas A. Bentley	
☐ Independent	John Galt, Jr.—Kay Lee	
☐ Light	Da Vid	
☐ United States Pacifist Party	Bradford Lyttle	

2004

☐	Republican	George W. Bush—Richard B. Cheney
☐	Democratic	John F. Kerry—John Edwards
☐	Independent	Ralph Nader—Peter M. Camejo
☐	Reform	Ralph Nader—Peter M. Camejo
☐	Libertarian	Michael Badnarik—Richard Campagna
☐	Constitution	Michael Peroutka—Chuck Baldwin
☐	Green	David Cobb—Pat LaMarche
☐	Socialist Workers	Roger Calero—Arrin Hawkins
☐	Socialist	Walter Brown—Mary Alice Herbert
☐	Workers World	John Parker—Teresa Gutierrez
☐	Personal Choice	Charles Jay—Marilyn Chambers
☐	Independent	Randall Venson—Gene Kelly
☐	Prohibition	Gene Amondson—Leroy Plettin
☐	Prohibition-Colorado faction	Earl Dodge—Howard Lydick
☐	Peace & Freedom	Leonard Peltier—Barry Bachrach
☐	American Party	Diane Templin—Al Moore
☐	Socialist Equality	Bill Van Auken—Jim Lawrence

Appendix 3: Alphabetical list of Presidential Hopefuls

The following is a list of most people who were considered contenders for the presidency since 1789. Campaign items for presidential hopefuls are usually more valuable than those for candidates for lower offices. Using this list you can see if an item you come across is for a hopeful.

The letters R and D after the names indicate the party for which the person was considered a hopeful candidate. This is followed by the year in which they were considered.

A

Adams, John Quincy, 1828
Adams, Samuel, 1796
Ahern, Frank, D-1980
Alexander, Lamar, R-1996
Alger, Russell A., R-1888
Allen, William, D-1876
Allison, William, R-1888, 1896
Allott, Gordon, R-1964
Anderson, John, R-1980
Armstrong, James, 1789
Arnold, Gary, R-1984
Arnold, S. C., R-1956
Arthur, Chester A., R-1884
Ashbrook, John, R-1972
Askew, Reuben, D-1984
Ayres, William, D-1928

B

Babbitt, Bruce, D-1988
Babcock, Edward, R-1916
Bacon, Augustus, D-1908
Badgley, Donald, R-1980
Baker, Howard, R-1980
Baker, James, R-1996
Baker, Newton, D-1920, 1924, 1932
Baldwin, Raymond, R-1948
Baldwin, Simeon, D-1912
Bankhead, William, D-1940
Banks, Nathaniel, R-1856
Barkley, Alben, D-1952
Barnes, Roy, D-2004
Barnett, Ross, D-1960
Bartlett, Dewey, R-1968
Barton, Bruce, R-1940
Bates, Edward, R-1856, 1860
Battle, John, D-1956
Bauer, Gary, R-2000
Bayard, Thomas F., D-1872, 1876, 1880, 1884
Bayh, Birch, D-1976
Beckwith, Frank, R-1960
Behrman, M., D-1924
Belluso, Nick, R-1980
Bender, Riley, R-1944, 1948, 1952
Bennett, William, R-1996

Bentley, H. O., D-1932
Bentsen, Lloyd, D-1976
Beveridge, Albert, R-1912
Biden, Joseph, D-1988, 2004
Bilbo, Theodore, D-1928
Black, Jeremiah S., D-1872, 1880
Black, John Charles, D-1896
Blackburn, Joseph, D-1896
Blaine, James G, R-1876, 1880, 1888, 1892
Blaine, John, R-1932
Blair, Francis P., D-1868
Bland, Richard, D-1896
Bliss, Cornelius, R-1896
Bocock, Thomas S., D-1860
Boies, Horace, D-1896
Boles, Horace, D-1892
Borah, William, R-1916, 1920, 1936
Bowles, Chester, D-1960
Boyd, Linn, D-1852
Bradley, Bill, D-2000, 2004
Bradley, William, R-1896
Branigin, Roger, D-1968
Braun, Carol Moseley, D-2004
Breckinridge, John C., D-1860
Brewster, Bob, D-1984
Brewster, Daniel, D-1964
Bricker, John, R-1944, 1956
Bridges, Henry Styles, R-1940
Bristow, Benjamin H., R-1876
Broadhead, James O., D-1876
Brown, Edmund G. "Pat", D-1952, 1960
Brown, Fred, D-1924
Brown, Jerry, D-1976, 1980, 1992
Brumbaugh, Martin, R-1916
Bryan, Charles W., D-1920
Bryan, William Jennings, D-1912, 1920
Buchanan, James, D-1844, 1848, 1852,
Buchanan, Pat, R-1996
Buckley, William, R-1976
Bulkley, Robert, D-1952
Burke, John, D-1912
Burr, Aaron, 1792
Burton, Theodore, R-1916, 1924
Bush, George H. W., R-1980
Bushfield, Harlan, R-1940

Edwards, John, D-2004
Eisenhower, Dwight D., D-1948
Eisenhower, Edgar, R-1960
Eisenhower, Milton, R-1960
Ellsworth, Oliver, 1796
English, James E., D-1868, 1880
Ewing, Oscar, D-1952
Ewing, Thomas, D-1880

F

Fairbanks, Charles, R-1908, 1916
Farley, James, D-1940, 1944
Faubus, Orval, D-1960
Fauntroy, Walter E., D-1972
Feingold, Russ, D-2004
Feinstein, Dianne, D-2004
Fernandez, Ben, R-1980, 1984, 1988
Ferris, Woodbridge, D-1924
Field, Stephen J., D-1880
Fillmore, Millard, W-1852
Filoa, Neil K., R-1976, 1980
Finch, Cliff, D-1980
Fish, Hamilton, Jr., R-1896
Fisher, Paul, D-1960, R-1960
Fitler, Edwin H., R-1888
Flower, Roswell P., D-1884
Floyd, John, 1832
Folk, Joseph W., D-1908
Fong, Hiram, R-1964, 1968
Foraker, Joseph, R-1888, 1908
Forbes, Malcolm S. (Steve), R-1996, 2000
Ford, Gerald, R-1980
Ford, Henry, R-1916, D-1924
Foss, Eugene, D-1912
France, Joseph, R-1932
Fremont, John C., R-1860
Fulbright, J. William, D-1952, 1968
Fuller, Alvan, R-1928
Fuller, Melville W., D-1908

G

Gannett, Frank, R-1940
Garner, John Nance, D-1932, 1940
Gaynor, William, D-1908, 1912
George, Walter, D-1928
Gephardt, Richard, D-1988, 2004
Gerard, James, D-1920, 1924
Gingrich, Newt, R-1996
Glass, Carter, D-1920, 1924
Glenn, John, D-1984
Goff, Guy, R-1928
Goldwater, Barry, R-1960, 1968
Gore, Albert Jr., D-1988, 2004
Gorman, Arthur P., D-1892, 1904
Graham, Bob, D-2004

Gramm, Phil, R-1996
Grant, Frederick D., R-1888
Grant, Ulysses S., R-1864, 1880
Gray, George, D-1904, 1908
Gray, James, D-1968
Green, Dwight, R-1948
Green, Warren, R-1936
Gregor, M. C., R-1920
Gresham, Walter Q., R-1888
Griser, Robert, D-1984
Groesbeck, William S., D-1872
Guthrie, James, D-1860

H

Hadley, Herbert, R-1912
Haig, Alexander, R-1988
Hamilton, Lee, R-1992, 2000
Hancock, John, 1789
Hancock, Winfield Scott, D-1876
Hanna, Marcus, R-1904
Harbord, James, R-1924
Harding, Warren G., R-1916
Harkin, Tom, D-1992
Harmon, Jacob, R-1920
Harmon, Judson, D-1904, 1908, 1912
Harriman, W. Averell, D-1952, 1956
Harris, Fred, D-1972, 1976
Harrison, Benjamin, R-1896
Harrison, Byron, D-1924, 1928
Harrison, Francis, D-1920
Harrison, Robert, 1789
Harrison, William H., 1836
Hart, Gary, D-1984, 1988, 2004
Hartke, Vance, D-1972
Hartranft, John F., R-1876
Hatch, Orrin, R-2000
Hawley, Joseph R., R-1884, 1888
Hay, John, R-1904
Hayes, William, R-1920
Haymond, Creed, R-1888
Hays, Wayne, D-1972
Hearst, William Randolph, D-1904, 1920, 1932
Henderson, Leon, D-1948
Hendricks, Thomas A., D-1868, 1876, 1880, 1884
Henry, John, 1796
Herter, Christian, R-1956
Hildebrandt, Fred, D-1944
Hill, David B., D-1892, 1896
Hitchcock, Gilbert, D-1920, 1928
Hoadly, George, D-1884
Holdridge, Herbert, D-1948
Hollings, Ernest, D-1984
Hoover, Herbert, R-1920, 1924, 1936, 1940
Houston, David, D-1924
Houston, Samuel, D-1852

Hughes, Charles Evans, R-1908, 1912, 1928
Hughes, Harold, D-1972
Hull, Cordell, D-1924, 1928, 1940
Humphrey, Hubert H., D-1952, 1960, 1972, 1976
Hunter, Robert M. T., D-1860
Huntington, Samuel, 1789

I

Iacocca, Lee, D-1988
Ingalls, John J., R-1888
Ingersoll, R. J., 1852
Iredell, James, 1796

J

Jackson, Andrew, 1824
Jackson, Henry, D-1972, 1976
Jackson, Jesse, D-1984, 1988, 1996
Jackson, Jesse, Jr., D-2004
Jacobsen, Alvin, R-1980
James, Arthur, R-1940
James, Ollie, D-1912
Jay, John, 1789, 1796
Jefferson, Thomas, 1792
Jewell, Marshall, R-1876
Jewett, Hugh J., D-1880
Johnson, Andrew, D-1860, 1868
Johnson, Hiram, R-1920, 1924, 1932
Johnson, John, D-1908
Johnson, Lyndon B., D-1956, 1960, 1968
Johnson, Reverdy, D-1868
Johnson, Richard M., D-1844
Johnson, Samuel, 1796
Johnson, Tom, D-1904, 1908
Jones, Jesse, D-1928
Jones, Walter, D-1956
Judd, Walter, R-1960, 1964

K

Kaptur, Marcy, D-2004
Kay, Richard, D-1980, 1984
Kefauver, Estes, D-1952, 1956, 1960
Kelley, David, R-1984
Kelley, V. A., R-1980
Kellogg, Frank, R-1920
Kemp, Jack, R-1980, 1988, 1996
Kendrick, John, D-1924
Kennedy, Edward M., D-1968, 1972, 1976, 1980, 1984
Kennedy, Robert F., D-1964, 1968
Kenyon, WIlliam, R-1924
Kern, John, D-1912
Kerr, Robert, D-1952
Kerrey, Bob, D-1992, 2004
Kerry, John, D-2004
Keyes, Alan, R-1996, 2000
King, Rufus, 1816

Kirk, Claude, D-1968
Kirkpatrick, Jeane, R-1988
Knowland, William F., R-1956
Knox, Frank, R-1936
Knox, Philander R-1908, 1916, 1920
Koczak, Stephen, D-1984
Kucinich, Dennis, D-2004

L

LaFollette, Robert, R-1908, 1912, 1916, 1920, 1924
LaGuardia, Fiorella, R-1940
Lane, Joseph, D-1852
Lanley, Ben, D-1948
Lardner, Ring, D-1920
LaRouche, Lyndon, Jr., D-1980-2004
Larsen, Scotty, D-1980
Lausche, Frank, D-1956
Laxalt, Paul, R-1988
Lenroot, Irvine, R-1920
Lewis Cass, D-1844, 1852, 1856
Lewis, James Hamilton, D-1932
Lewis, James, D-1912
Lieberman, Joseph, D-2004
Limbaugh, Rush, R-1996
Lincoln, Benjamin, 1789
Lincoln, Robert T., R-1884, 1888, 1892
Lindsay, John, R-1968, D-1972
Linger, Claude, D-1944
Linton, William, R-1896
Lodge, Henry Cabot, Jr., R-1960, 1964
Lodge, Henry Cabot, R-1916
Logan, John A., R-1884
Lothrop, George, D-1880
Loveland, W. A. H., D-1880
Loveless, Herschel, D-1960
Lowden, Frank, R-1920, 1924, 1928
Lucas, Scott, D-1948

M

MacArthur, Douglas, R-1944, 1948, 1952
MacNider, Hanford, R-1940
Maddox, Bob, D-1980
Maddox, Lester, D-1968
Magnuson, Warren, D-1956
Mangum, William P., 1836
Mann, James Robert, R-1916
Marcy, William L., D-1852
Marshall, Thomas, D-1912, 1920, 1924
Martin, Joseph W., Jr., R-1940, 1948
Martin, Edward, R-1948
Matthews, Claude, D-1896
McAdoo, Thomas W., D-1928
McAdoo, William Gibbs, D-1920, 1924, 1932
McCain, John, R-2000
McCall, Samuel, R-1916

McCarthy, Eugene, D-1968, 1972, 1976, 1992
McClean, John, W-1848
McClellan, George, D-1904
McClelland, George B., D-1880
McCloskey, Paul, R-1972
McCormack, Ellen, D-1976
McCormack, John, D-1956
McCormack, Robert, R-1944
McDonald, Joseph E., D-1880, 1884
McGovern, George, D-1968, 1984
McKinley, William, R-1888, 1892
McLain, George, D-1960
McLean, John, D-1896
McLean, John, R-1856, 1860
McMahon, Brien (Jason O'Brien), D-1952
McNary, Charles, R-1940
McNutt, Paul, D-1940, 1948
Meredith, Edwin, D-1920, 1924
Meyner, Robert, D-1960
Miles, Nelson, D-1904
Mills, Wilbur, D-1972
Milton, John, 1789
Mink, Patsy, D-1972
Mondale, Walter, D-1972
Moore, Dan, D-1968
Morrison, William R., D-1880, 1892, 1896
Morse, Wayne, R-1952
Morton, Levi, R-1896
Morton, Oliver P., R-1876
Murphy, Frank, D-1940
Murray, James, D-1952
Murray, William H., D-1932
Muskie, Edmund S., D-1956, 1972, 1976, 1980

N

Nader, Ralph, D-1992
Nice, Harry, R-1936
Nixon, Richard, R-1956, 1964
Norris, George S., R-1928, 1932
Nunn, Sam, D-1988

O

O'Connor, Charles, D-1864
O'Connor, Sandra Day, R-1984
O'Mahoney, Joseph, D-1948
Olney, Richard, D-1904
Owen, Robert, D-1920, 1924

P

Packer, Asa, D-1868
Palmer, A. Mitchell, D-1920
Parker, Joel, D-1868, 1876, 1880
Patterson, Ellis, D-1940
Pattison, Robert E., D-1892, 1896, 1904
Paulsen, Pat, D-1968, 1972, 1988, 1992, 1996

Payne, Henry B., D-1880
Pearce, James A., D-1860
Peckham, Rufus, D-1908
Pendleton, George H., D-1868
Pennoyer, Sylvestor, D-1896
Pepper, Claude, D-1948, 1952
Percy, Charles, R-1968, 1976
Pershing, Gen. John, R-1920
Phelps, William W., R-1888
Phillips, Channing, D-1968
Pierce, Franklin, D-1856
Pinkney, Thomas, 1796, 1800, 1804, 1808
Poindexter, Miles, R-1920
Pomerene, Atlee, D-1920, 1928
Porter, Albert, D-1964
Powell, Colin, D-1996
Pritchard, Jeter, R-1920

Q

Quay, Matthew, R-1896
Quayle, Dan, R-1996

R

Ralston, Samuel, D-1924
Randall, Samuel J., D-1880, 1884
Rayburn, Sam, D-1952
Reagan, Ronald, R-1968, 1976
Reaux, Don, D-1980
Reece, Brazilla, R-1948
Reed, James, D-1928, 1932
Reed, John M., R-1860
Reed, Thomas B., R-1892, 1896
Reich, Robert, D-2004
Reynolds, John, D-1964
Rhodes, James, R-1964, 1968
Ritchie, Albert C., D-1924, 1932
Robertson, Pat, R-1988
Robinson, Joseph, D-1924, 1932
Rockefeller, Jay, D-1992
Rockefeller, Nelson, R-1960, 1964, 1968
Rockefeller, Winthrop, R-1968
Roden, George, D-1976
Rogers, Will, D-1932
Rollinson, Ray, D-1976, 1980, 1984, 1988
Romney, George, R-1964, 1968
Roosevelt, Theodore, R-1908, 1912, 1916
Root, Elihu, R-1916
Rosellini, Albert, D-1960
Ross, Robert, R-1928
Rusk, Jeremiah M., R-1888
Russell, Richard, D-1948, 1952
Russell, William E., D-1892, 1896
Rutledge, John, 1789

S

Sanderson, Daniel, D-1980
Sanford, Terry, D-1972, 1976
Saulsbury, Willard, D-1924
Schroeder, Pat, D-1988
Scott, Winfield, W-1840, 1848
Scranton, William, R-1964, 1968
Seward, William, R-1856, 1860
Seymour, Horatio, D-1860, 1864, 1880
Seymour, Thomas H., D-1864
Shafer, Raymond, R-1968
Shapp, Milton, D-1976
Sharpton, Al, D-2004
Shellenberg, Tom, D-1996
Sherman, John, R-1880, 1884, 1888
Sherman, Lawrence Y., R-1916
Sherman, William T., R-1884
Shriver, Sargent, D-1976
Silzer, George, D-1924
Simmons, Furnifold, D-1920
Simon, Paul, D-1988
Smathers, George, D-1960, 1968
Smith, Alfred E., D-1920, 1924, 1932
Smith, Margaret Chase, R-1964
Specter, Arlen, D-1996
Sproul, William, R-1920
Stassen, Harold, R-1944-1984
Stevenson, Adlai E. I, D-1892, 1896
Stevenson, Adlai E. II, D-1960, 1964
Stewart, Commodore, D-1844
Sulzer, William, D-1912
Sumner, Charles, R-1856, 1860
Sutherland, George, R-1920
Sutherland, Howard, R-1920
Sweet, William, D-1924
Symington, Stuart, D-1956, 1960

T

Taft, Robert, R-1936, 1940, 1948, 1952
Taft, William Howard, R-1916
Taylor, Morry, D-1996
Telfair, Edward, 1789
Teller, Henry, D-1896
Thompson, Houston, D-1924, 1928
Thompson, Tommy, D-1996
Thurman, Allen G., D-1876, 1880, 1884
Thurmond, Strom, R-1968
Tilden, Samuel J., D-1880, 1844
Tillman, Benjamin, D-1896
Timinski, Alfred, D-1984
Timmerman, George, Jr., D-1956
Toucey, Isaac, D-1860
Tower, John, R-1968
Towne, Charles, D-1904

Traylor, Melvin, D-1932
Truman, Harry, D-1952
Tsongas, Paul, D-1992
Turpie, David, D-1896
Tydings, Millard, D-1940

U

Udall, Morris, D-1976
Underwood, Oscar, D-1912, 1920, 1924
Unruh, Jesse, D-1968

V

Vandenberg, Arthur, R-1936, 1940, 1948
Vilsack, Tom, D-2004
Volpe, John, R-1968
Vauclain, Samuel, R-1920

W

Wade, Benjamin F., R-1860
Wadsworth, James, R-1932
Waldbridge, Cyrus, R-1904
Wall, Edward, D-1904
Wallace, George C., D-1964, 1968, 1972, 1976
Wallace, Henry, D-1948
Walsh, Matthew, D-1964
Walsh, Thomas, D-1924
Wanamaker, John, R-1916
Warner, William, R-1908
Warren, Charles, R-1920
Warren, Earl, R-1936, 1944, 1948, 1952
Warren, Francis, R-1920
Washburne, Elihu B., R-1876, 1880
Washington, George, 1796
Watson, James, R-1920, 1924, 1928
Watts, Richard, D-1928
Webster, Daniel, W-1836, 1848, 1852
Weeks, John W., R-1916
Weller, J. B., D-1852
Werdel, Thomas, R-1952
Westmoreland, William, Gen., D-1968
Wheeler, Burton K., D-1940
Wheeler, William A., R-1876
White, Edward, D-1908
White, George, D-1932
White, Hugh L., 1836
Whitman, Charles, R-1916
Whitney, William C., D-1892
Wilder, Douglas, D-1992
Williams, Betty Jean, D-1984
Williams, G. Mennen, D-1952
Williams, John, D-1904, 1908, 1920
Willis, Frank, R-1916, 1928
Willis, Gerald, D-1984
Willkie, Wendell, R-1944

Appendix 4: Political Initials & Acronyms

The following is a list of slogans and acronyms used on presidential campaign items in the last century which have obscure meanings. This list will help you determine if a button with an unusual slogan was from a presidential campaign.

ABB	Anybody But Bush (2004)
ABC	Anybody But Carter (1980)
ABC	Anybody But Clinton (1996)
ABJ	Anybody But Johnson (1968)
ABK	Anybody But Kennedy (1968, 1980)
ACTWU	American Clothing and Textile Workers Union
ACWA	Amalgamated Clothing Workers of America
ADA	Americans for Democratic Action
AFGE	American Federation of Government Employees
AFL-CIO	American Federation of Labor-Congress of Industrial Organizations
AFSCME	American Federation of State, County& Municipal Employees
AFT	American Federation of Teachers
AIP	American Independent Party
ALP	American Labor Party
AuH_2O	Chemical formula for Goldwater
BAM	Black American Movement (McCarthy 1968)
BGB	Barry Goldwater Backer (1964)
BMG	Barry M. Goldwater (1964)
BRAC	Brotherhood of Railway & Airline Clerks
CC	Calvin Coolidge (1924)
CDA	Coalition for a Democratic Alternative
CDC	California Democratic Council
C5H4N4O3	Formula for Urine ("C5H4N4O3 on AuH2O" anti-Goldwater 1964)
CIC	Coalition for a Independant Candidacy (McCarthy 1968)
C.I.D.W.I.	Central Illinois Democratic Women, Inc.
CRL	Connecticut Republican League
C/M	Carter - Mondale (1976,1980)
COPE	Committee on Political Education
CPUSA	Communist Party of the U.S.A.
CTA/NEA	California Teachers Assn./National Education Assn.
CWA	Communications Workers of America
CWA	Russian (Cyrillic) letters for USA
DFL	Democratic Farmer Labor
DFR	Defeat Franklin Roosevelt
DNC	Democratic National Committee
DNC	Democratic National Convention
DWG	Distillery Workers Guild
EMc2	Eugene McCarthy a 2nd time (1972)
EMK	Edward M. Kennedy
ESM	Edmund Sixtus Muskie
FBBI	For Bush Before Iowa (1980)
FCBNH	For Carter Before New Hampshire (1976)
FDP	Freedom Democratic Party
FDR	Franklin D. Roosevelt
FEF	Forget Eisenhower Forever (1956)
FKBW	For Kennedy Before Wisconsin (1960)
FMBDNC	For McGovern Before the Democratic National Convention

FMBM	For McGovern Before Miami
FMBNH	For McCarthy Before New Hampshire (1968)
FMBNH	For McGovern Before New Hampshire (1972)
F3C	Rule F(3)(c) requiring democratic delegates to vote for candidate they were elected for (1980)
G	Goldwater (1964)
GMG	George McGovern
GOP	Grand Old Party (Republican)
HG	Hoover and Green (Michigan candidate)
HHH	Hubert Horatio Humphrey (1968)
H3	Hubert Horatio Humphrey (1968)
IAK	I Adore Kennedy (1960)
IAM	International Association of Machinists
IDC/NDC	Illinois Democratic Coalition/National Democratic Coalition
IBEW	International Brotherhood of Electrical Workers
IB of TCS&H	International Brotherhood of Teamsters, Chauffers, Stablemen & Helpers
IGHAT	I'm Gonna Hate All Trumans or I'm Gonna Holler About Taxes (1948)
IGHAT	Ike's Gotta Have Another Term (1956)
ILA	International Longshoreman's Assn.
ILGWU	International Ladies Garment Workers Union
IT	Ike Twice (1956)
IUE	International Union of Electricians
IUOE	International Union of Operating Engineers
IVI	Independent Voters of Illinois
IWW	International Workers of the World
IYHYKHR	In Your Heart You Know He's Right (Goldwater 1964)
JC	Jimmy Carter (1976, 1980)
K7UGA in 64	Goldwater's CB license (1964)
K-J	Kennedy-Johnson (1960)
KMA	Kiss My Ass (McGovern 1972)
KNKC	Keep Nebraska Kennedy Conscious
La Tei YAaNi	Barry Goldwater's Name in Navajo (1964)
LBJ	Lyndon Baines Johnson
LNPL	Labor's Non-Partisan League
LOTE	Lesser of Two Evils (Carter 1980)
M Go Fritz	University of Michigan for Mondale (1984)
McG/25	McGovern/$25 donation (1972)
MEA /NEA	Minnesota Education Assn./Nat'l Education Assn.
MFWRO	Massachusetts Federation of Women Republican Organizations
N/A	Nixon & Agnew (1968, 1972)
NASW	National Association of Social Workers
NEA	National Education Association
NJEA/PAC	New Jersey Education Assn. / Political Action Committee
NOW	National Organization of Women
NSRP	National States' Rights Party
Oct.9th	Date Nixon gave a speech (McGovern 1972)
PAC	Political Action Committee
PFP	Peace & Freedom Party (1968)
PT 109	John F. Kennedy's WWII boat number (1960)
R&B	Reagan & Bush (1980, 1984)
RFK	Robert F. Kennedy
RIF	Reduction in Force (anti-Reagan, 1984)
RIJ	Republicans & Independant for Johnson (1964)
RJ	Roosevelt & Johnson (1912)
RK is OK by JC	Robert Kennedy is okay by James Carter (1968)

RNC	Republican National Committee
RNC	Republican National Convention
R & R	Reagan & Rockefeller (1968)
RR	Ronald Reagan
SEIU	Service Employees Internationl Union
SIE	Society of Industrial Engineers
SIN	Stop Inflation Now
SLP	Socialist Labor Party
SOB Club	Save Our Business Club (anti-JFK)
SPUSA	Socialist Party USA
SWP	Socialist Workers Party
TANSTAAFL	There Ain't No Such Thing as a Free Lunch (Hospers 1972)
TASK	Teen-Agers for Stevenson & Kefauver (1956)
TED 48	Thomas E. Dewey 1948
TGFMLU	Thank God for Mondale & Labor Unions
TIRCC	This Is Reagan Country Club
TMK	Too Many Kennedys (anti-EMK)
TR	Theodore Roosevelt
TRT	Taxpayers Revivalist Ticket
T.S.	Taft & Sherman
TTP	Tired Tax Payers
TUIT	To It as in "when I get around to it"
UAW	United Auto Workers
UFCW	United Food & Commercial Workers
UFT	United Federation of Teachers
UFW	United Farm Workers
UMWA	United Mine Workers of America
UPWA-CIO	Union Printing Workers Association
URFI	United Republican Fund of Illinois
URW	United Rubber Workers
USWA	United Steel Workers of America
UYN	United Youth for Nixon (1968)
VFBG	Vote for Barry Goldwater (1964)
VIP	Voice in Politics (Wallace 1968)
VV	Vietnam Veterans (McCarthy 1968)
W&M	Wilson & Marshall (1912, 1916)
WCTU	Women's Christian Temperance Union
WIN	Whip Inflation Now (Ford, 1974-1975)
YAF	Young Americans for Freedom
YAFK	Young Americans for Kennedy
YCERSOYA	You Can't Elect Republicans Sitting on Your Ass (or Aft) (1950s)
YD	Young Democrats
YP	Young Professionals
YPR	Young Professionals for Reagan
YRC	Young Republican Clubs
3G/B	George Bush (represents polls showing 3% support)
3H	Hubert Horatio Humphrey
4JKB4IA	For John Kerry Before Iowa
8(Ball)	Behind the 8 Ball (anti-FDR 1940, anti-Truman 1948)
16 to 1	Proposed silver to gold ratio (Bryan 1896, 1900)
26 million club	Goldwater's vote total (1964)
60 (on a "V")	Oregon button for Kennedy 1960
50,001	Oregon primary vote for Dewey
250, 000	Young Republicans supporting Nixon

Occasionally you might come across an items which merely says something like "Vote Democratic Nov. 8th." By looking at the chart below and the approximate age of the item you can determine which election it is from and therefore which candidate it supports. This list begins in 1848 because that was the first year the presidential election was held on the same date throughout the country. Before that, states were allowed to hold the election any time in a 34 day period before the first Wednesday of December.

Keep in mind that municipal and state elections are also held in years between presidential elections.

Nov. 2	Election day, 1852, 1880, 1920, 1948, 1976, 2004
Nov. 3	Election day, 1868, 1896, 1908, 1936, 1964, 1992
Nov. 4	Election day, 1856, 1884, 1924, 1952, 1980, 2008
Nov. 5	Election day, 1872, 1912, 1940, 1968, 1996, 2012
Nov. 6	Election day, 1860, 1888, 1900, 1928, 1956, 1984
Nov. 7	Election day, 1848, 1876, 1916, 1944, 1972, 2000
Nov. 8	Election day, 1864, 1892, 1904, 1932, 1960, 1988

Index